Dress Up Dolls

Amigurumi Crochet Patterns

By Sayjai Thawornsupacharoen

From the series : Sayjai's Amigurumi Crochet Patterns, volume 3
K and J Publishing, 16 Whitegate Close, Swavesey, Cambridge CB24 4TT, England

Contents

Doll Patterns

18 Tiny Teddy Bear
20 Basic Doll Pattern
23 Lilly Doll
25 Evie Doll
27 Boy Doll
29 Bear Doll
31 Bunny Doll

Clothing

33 Underpants
34 Bikini
36 Swim Shorts
49 Pyjamas
50 Sun Dress
52 Dungarees Dress
54 Dungarees
56 Christmas Dress
60 Shrug & Scarf
62 Shoulder Straps Dress
64 Bell Shaped Dresses
68 Red Riding Hood Cape
71 White Top
72 Skirt
73 Shorts
74 Blue Top
75 Trousers
76 Jacket

Hats

43 Christmas Hat
45 Sleeping Hat
47 Sun Hat
48 Cap

Shoes

38 Boots
39 Slippers
40 Mary Jane Shoes
41 Ballet Pumps
42 Trainers

Bags

79 Messenger Bag
80 Square Bag
80 Circle Bag
81 Beach Bag
83 Big Carry Bag

82 Watering Can

22 How to: Cloth Hanger
85 How to join Yarn
85 How to read pattern
86 Yarn Weight System
87 Crochet Hook Conversion Chart

Bunny Doll -> P. 31
Lilly Doll -> P. 23
Bear Doll -> P. 29
Boy Doll -> P. 27
Evie Doll -> P. 25

Bikini -> P. 34
Swim Shorts -> P. 36
Beach Bag -> P. 81

Dungarees -> P. 54
Sun Hat -> P. 47

Cap -> P. 48
Trainers -> P. 42

Mary Jane Shoes -> P. 40
Watering Can -> P. 82

Shoulder Straps Dress -> P. 62
Square Bag -> P. 80

Sun Dress -> P. 50

Long Bell Shaped Dress -> P. 65

Short Bell Shaped Dress -> P. 67

Red Riding Hood Cape -> P. 68

White Top -> P. 71
Shorts -> P. 73
Skirt -> P. 72
Messenger Bag -> P. 79

Dungarees Dress -> P. 52

Ballet Pumps Shoes -> P. 41

Sleeping Hat -> P. 45
Pyjamas -> P. 49
Tiny Teddy Bear -> P. 18
Slippers -> P. 39

Blue Top -> P. 74
Jacket -> P. 76

Trousers -> P. 75
Shoes -> P. 42

Christmas Hat -> P. 43
Christmas Dress -> P. 56

Shrug -> P. 60
Boots -> P. 38

Big Carry Bag -> P. 83

Introduction

The Dress Up Dolls are very cute, huggable and can change clothes, shoes and hats. They have a tiny teddy bear and sets of dresses, shoes, hats and bags. Also included is the pattern for the big bag to carry and keep them tidy. The dolls are made by using single crochet stitch (UK: double crochet). Crochet 2 strands of DK yarn together and use a 5 mm hook. The dresses are made by crocheting one strand of DK yarn with a 4 mm hook.

Use 2 strands of yarn to make the dolls, so the dolls can be made quickly. Use one strand of yarn to make the dresses, so the dresses are not too thick or stiff.

Size

- The dolls are about 16 inches/ 41.5 cm tall standing.
- The Tiny Teddy Bear is 2.5 inches/ 6.5 cm tall standing.

Abbreviations

The Dress Up Doll patterns use USA crochet terminology.
ch = chain
sc = single crochet
hdc = half double crochet
dc = double crochet
st = stitch
sl = slip
rnd = round
tog = together

Conversion chart for USA/ UK crochet abbreviations:

USA Crochet Abbreviations	UK Crochet Abbreviations
sc = single crochet	dc = double crochet
hdc = half double crochet	htr = half treble crochet
dc = double crochet	tr = treble crochet

Tools

- Crochet hooks: 4 mm hook (US: G/6, UK: 8), 5 mm hook (US: H/8, UK: 6) and 6 mm hook (US: J/10, UK: 4)
- Stitch markers
- Yarn needle
- Sewing needle
- Pins
- Scissors

Yarn

- DK, Light Worsted 

- Chunky, Bulky 

Gauge

4 mm hook and one strand of DK yarn
Single crochet: 20 sts = 4" (10 cm)
25 rows = 4" (10cm)
Double crochet: 18 sts = 4" (10 cm)
10 rows = 4" (10cm)

5 mm hook and two strands of DK yarn
Single crochet: 14 sts = 4" (10 cm)
15 rows = 4" (10cm)

6 mm hook and one strand of Chunky yarn
Single crochet: 13 sts = 4" (10 cm)
14 rows = 4" (10cm)

For the first round: you can do 6 sc in magic ring instead of "Ch 2, 6 sc in second chain from hook."

Tiny Teddy Bear

Materials

- DK, Light Worsted (3 Light)
  1. Robin DK Taupe 093 = 10 g
  2. Cygnet Pato DK Blue 911 = 10 g
- Chunky, Bulky (5 Bulky)
  Schachenmayr Nomotta Cassiopeia, color White = 1 g for 2 scarfs
- 4 mm hook (US: G/6, UK: 8)
- 5 mm hook (US: H/8, UK: 6)
- DMC Pearl Cotton Thread Size 3 (115/3): Color Black 310 to embroider mouth
- Four of 4 mm black beads for eyes
- Needle and thread for attaching eyes
- Tapestry needle
- Polyester fibrefill = 10g for 2 Bears
- Stitch markers

Size

The Teddy Bears are 2.5"/ 6.5 cm tall standing.

Remarks

The Teddy Bear is crocheted using one strand of DK yarn and a 4 mm hook. Blue and Brown Bears are made with the same instructions

Leg

Make 2.

Rnd 1: With **Taupe 093**, ch 2, 6 sc in second chain from hook. (6)
Rnd 2-3: Sc in each st around. (6)

For first leg, join with sl st in first st. Fasten off.
For second leg, do not sl st in first st. Do not fasten off.

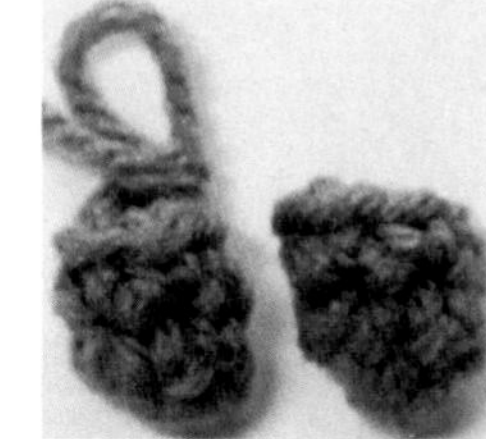

Body and Head

Rnd 1: Hold legs together with upper inner thighs together. Insert hook in the center on innermost thigh of first leg, pull out the loop from second leg, sc in same st (do not count this stitch: just for connecting legs together), sc in next 5 sts on second leg (mark first st), sc in next 5 sts on first leg. (10)

The sc is for connecting legs together and go through both legs. The next sc only go through second leg, then go round.

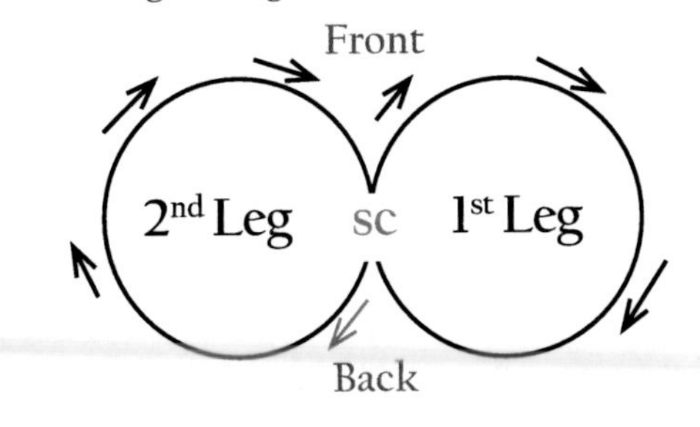

Rnd 2-4: Sc in each st around. Stuff. (10)
Rnd 5: Sc next 2 sts tog around. (5)
Rnd 6: 3 sc in each st around. (15)
Rnd 7: (Sc in next 2 sts, 2 sc in next st) around. (20)
Rnd 8-10: Sc in each st around. (20)
Rnd 11: (Sc in next 2 sts, sc next 2 sts tog) around. (15)
Rnd 12: (Sc next 2 sts tog, sc in next st) around. Stuff. (10)
Rnd 13: Sc next 2 sts tog around, sl st in first st, leave long end for sewing, fasten off. Sew opening close. (5)

Arm

Make 2, do not stuff.

Rnd 1: With **Taupe 093**, ch 2, 5 sc in second chain from hook. (5)
Rnd 2: Sc in each st around. (5)
Rnd 3: Sc in each st around, join with sl st in first st. Leave long end for sewing, fasten off. Sew arms to body.

Ear

Make 2.

Rnd 1: With **Taupe 093**, ch 2, 5 sc in second chain from hook. (5)
Rnd 2: Sc in each st around, join with sl st in first st. Leave long end for sewing, fasten off.

Scarf

With one strand of **Cassiopeia color White** and 5 mm hook, ch 20, fasten off.

Finishing

Sew ear on rnds 10-12 of head. Sew eyes 3 sts apart between rnds 9-10. With DMC Pearl Cotton Thread color **Black** embroider mouth (X between eyes).

Basic Doll Pattern

Remarks

The doll is crocheted using a 5 mm hook and two strands of DK yarn. 3 Light

Size

The dolls are about 16 inches/ 41.5 cm standing.

Head

Rnd 1: With two strands of DK yarn and 5 mm hook, ch 2, 6 sc in second chain from hook. (6)
Rnd 2: 2 sc in each st around. (12)
Rnd 3: (2 sc in next st, sc in next st) around. (18)
Rnd 4: (Sc in next 2 sts, 2 sc in next st) around. (24)
Rnd 5: (Sc in next 3 sts, 2 sc in next st) around. (30)
Rnd 6: Sc in next 2 sts, 2 sc in next st, (sc in next 4 sts, 2 sc in next st) 5 times, sc in next 2 sts. (36)
Rnd 7: (Sc in next 5 sts, 2 sc in next st) around. (42)
Rnd 8-13: Sc in each st around.
Rnd 14: (Sc next 2 sts tog, sc in next 5 sts) around. (36)
Rnd 15: Sc in next 2 sts, sc next 2 sts tog, (sc in next 4 sts, sc next 2 sts tog) 5 times, sc in next 2 sts. (30)
Rnd 16: (Sc in next 3 sts, sc next 2 sts tog) around. (24)
Rnd 17: (Sc in next 2 sts, sc next 2 sts tog) around. (18)
Rnd 18: (Sc in next 4 sts, sc next 2 sts tog) around, join with sl st in first st, fasten off. (15)

Stuff head a little bit, insert safety eyes 7 sts apart between rnds 11-12 of head, then stuff head more tightly.

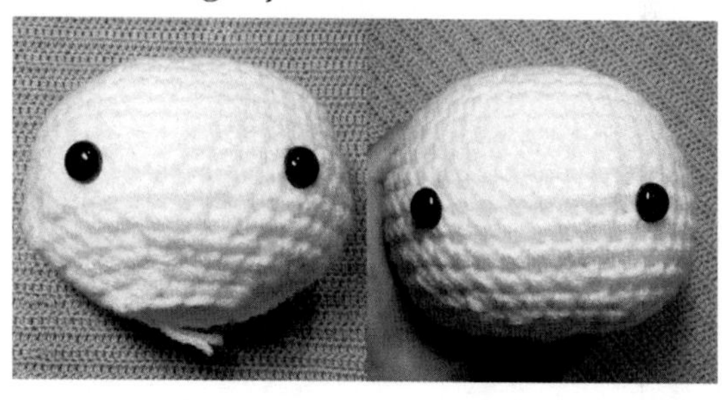

With **Red embroidery thread** embroider mouth (except Bear and Bunny).

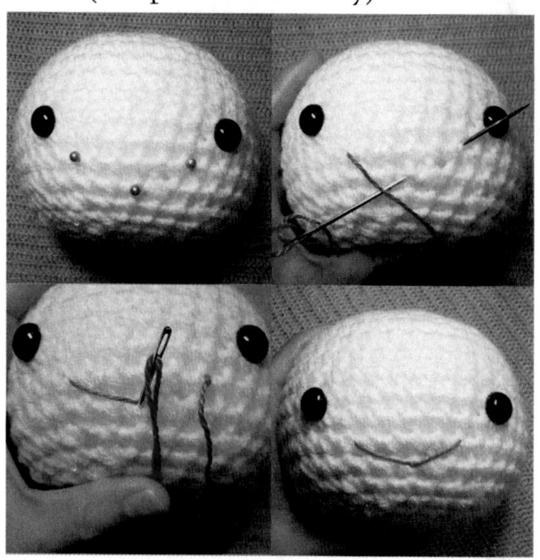

Body

Rnd 1: With 2 strands of DK yarn and 5 mm hook, ch 2, 6 sc in second chain from hook. (6)
Rnd 2: 2 sc in each st around. (12)
Rnd 3: (2 sc in next st, sc in next st) around. (18)

Rnd 4: (Sc in next 2 sts, 2 sc in next st) around. (24)
Rnd 5: (Sc in next 3 sts, 2 sc in next st) around. (30)
Rnd 6-11: Sc in each st around. (30)
Rnd 12: (Sc next 2 sts tog, sc in next 8 sts) around. (27)
Rnd 13: Sc in each st around.
Rnd 14: (Sc in next 7 sts, sc next 2 sts tog) around. (24)
Rnd 15: Sc in each st around. (24)
Rnd 16: Sc in next 3 sts, sc next 2 sts tog, (sc in next 6 sts, sc next 2 sts tog) 2 times, sc in next 3 sts. (21)
Rnd 17: Sc in each st around.
Rnd 18: (Sc next 2 sts tog, sc in next 5 sts) around. (18)
Rnd 19: Sc in each st around. (18)
Rnd 20: Sc in next 2 sts, sc next 2 sts tog, (sc in next 4 sts, sc next 2 sts tog) 2 times, sc in next 2 sts, sl st in first st, leave long end for sewing, fasten off. (15)

Stuff body and sew to head.

Foot and Leg

Make 2.

Rnd 1: With 2 strands of DK yarn and 5 mm hook, ch 7, sc in second chain from hook, sc in next 4 chs, 3 sc in last ch; working in remaining loops on opposite side of chain, sc in next 4 chs, 2 sc in next ch. (14)

X X X X X X O
X O O O O O O X
X X X X X X

o = chain x = sc

Rnd 2: 2 sc in next st, sc in next 4 sts, 2 sc in next 3 sts, sc in next 4 sts, 2 sc in next 2 sts. (20)
Rnd 3: Sc in next st, 2 sc in next st, sc in next 5 sts, 2 sc in next st, (sc in next st, 2 sc in next st) 2 times, sc in next 5 sts, 2 sc in next st, sc in next st, 2 sc in next st. (26)
Rnd 4-5: Sc in each st around. (26)
Rnd 6: Sc in next 8 sts, sc next 2 sts tog, (sc in next st, sc next 2 sts tog) 2 times, sc in next 10 sts. (23)
Rnd 7: Sc in next 8 sts, (sc next 2 sts tog) 3 times, sc in next 9 sts. (20)
Rnd 8: Sc in next 5 sts, (sc next 2 sts tog) 2 times, sc in next st, (sc next 2 sts tog) 2 times, sc in next 6 sts. (16)
Rnd 9: Sc in next 3 sts, (sc next 2 sts tog) 2 times, sc in next st, (sc next 2 sts tog) 2 times, sc in next 4 sts. Stuff. (12)
Rnd 10-27: Sc in each st around. (12)
Rnd 28: Sc in each st around, sl st in first st, leave long end for sewing, fasten off. Stuff legs a little bit, not too tight. Sew the opening close flat.

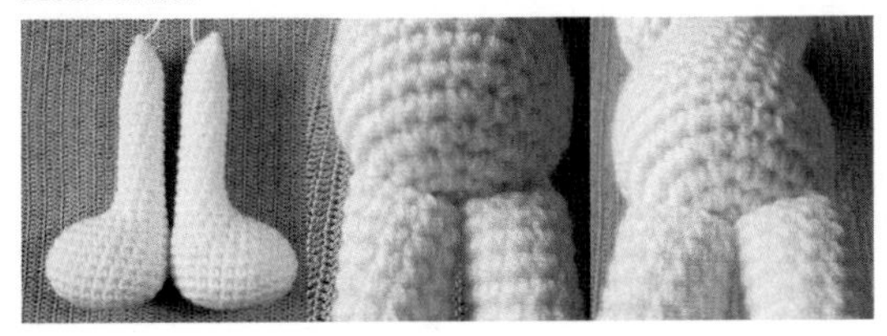

Do not stuff Body, Arms, Feet and Legs too tight. They will be soft, moveable (arms & legs) and the clothes will be easy to put on.

Arm

Make 2.

Rnd 1: With 2 strands of DK yarn [illegible] hook, ch 2, 6 sc in second chai[illegible]. (6)

Rnd 2: 2 sc in each st around. (12)

Rnd 3-5: Sc in each st around. (12)

Rnd 6: (Sc next 2 sts tog, sc in next 2 sts) around. Stuff. (9)

Rnd 7-19: Sc in each st around. (9)

Rnd 20: Sc in each st around, join with sl st in first st. Leave long end for sewing, fasten off. Stuff and sew arms to body.

Cloth Hanger

Cut iron wire 13 inches long, bend wire as in pictures.

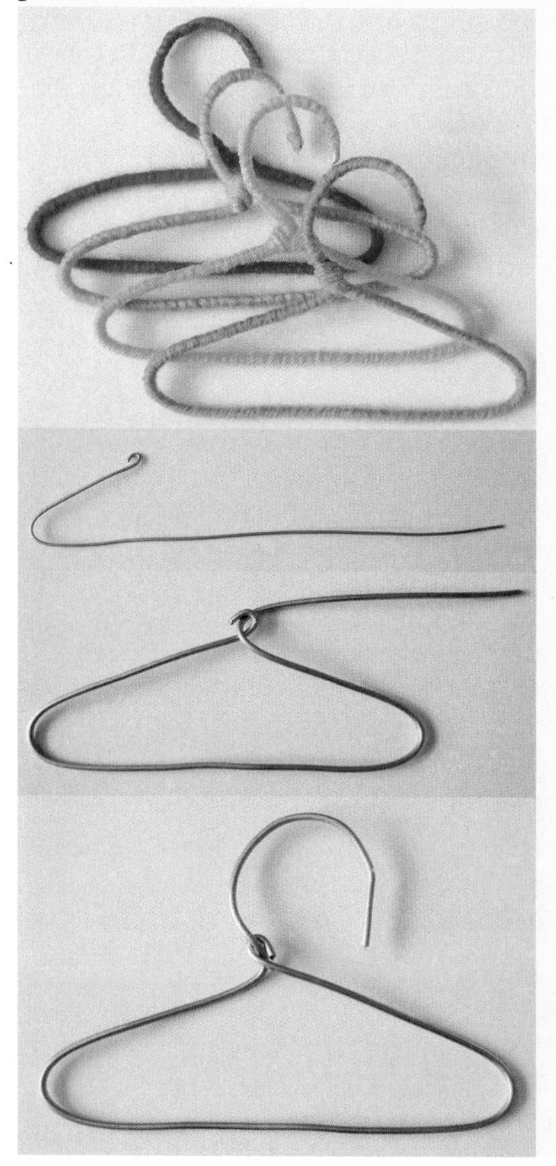

Cut the tip off a little bit.

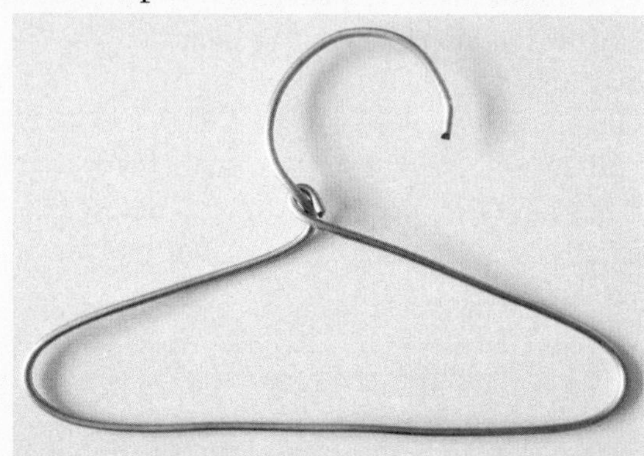

Wrap the yarn around the coat hanger. Use PVA glue at the beginning and end.

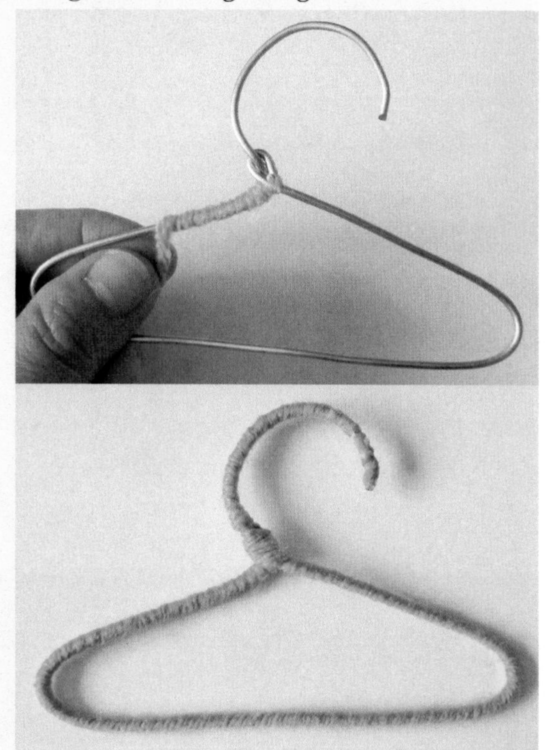

Lilly Doll

Doll

Make one same as Basic Doll pattern on page 20, use color **Cream 041** for all Body parts.

Materials

- DK, Light Worsted
  Robin DK: Cream 041 = 100 g and Acid yellow 060 = 40 g
- 5 mm hook (US: H/8, UK: 6)
- DMC Pearl Cotton Thread Size 3 (115/3): Color Red 321 to embroider mouth
- One pair of 12mm safety eyes
- 2 small red bows for decoration
- Tapestry needle
- Pins
- Polyester fibrefill = 135 g
- Stitch markers

Hair

Hair Cap

Rnd 1: With 2 strands of **Acid yellow 060** (hair color) and 5 mm hook, ch 2, 6 sc in second chain from hook. (6)
Rnd 2: 2 sc in each st around. (12)
Rnd 3: (2 sc in next st, sc in next st) around. (18)
Rnd 4: (Sc in next 2 sts, 2 sc in next st) around. (24)
Rnd 5: (Sc in next 3 sts, 2 sc in next st) around. (30)
Rnd 6: Sc in next 2 sts, 2 sc in next st, (sc in next 4 sts, 2 sc in next st) 5 times, sc in next 2 sts. (36)
Rnd 7: (Sc in next 5 sts, 2 sc in next st) around. (42)
Rnd 8: Sc in next 3 sts, 2 sc in next st, (sc in next 6 sts, 2 sc in next st) 5 times, sc in next 3 sts. (48)
Rnd 9-14: Sc in each st around. (48)

Rows 15-19 are working in rows.

Row 15: Sc in next 35 sts, turn. (35)

Row 16: Ch 1, sc in each st across, turn. (35)

Row 17: Ch 1, sc first 2 sts tog, sc in next 31 sts, sc next 2 sts tog, turn. (33)

Row 18: Ch 1, sc in each st across, turn. (33)

Row 19: Ch 1, sc first 2 sts tog, sc in next 29 sts, sc next 2 sts tog, leave long end for sewing, fasten off. (31)

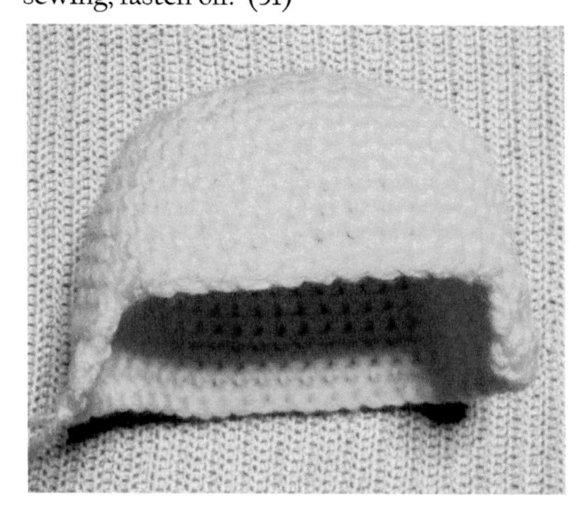

You can make pigtails or braids as you wish.

Put hair cap on head, pin it and sew to head. Cut 31 pieces of Yellow yarn, 12 inches (30 cm) long in length. For fringe, hold one strand of yarn, fold in half, insert hook in row 19 of hair cap, draw the folded end through the stitch and pull the loose ends through the folded end, draw the knot up tightly. Add 30 more. (See photos below.)

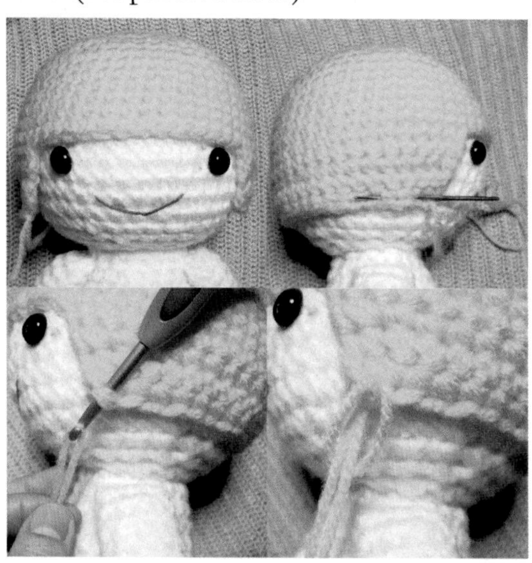

Evie Doll

Materials

- DK, Light Worsted
  Robin DK: Cream 041 = 85 g and Fiesta pink 064 = 20 g
- 5 mm hook (US: H/8, UK: 6)
- DMC Pearl Cotton Thread Size 3 (115/3) Color Red 321 for embroider mouth
- One pair of 12mm safety eyes
- Tapestry needle
- Pins
- Polyester fibrefill = 135 g
- Stitch markers

Doll

Body, Arms and Legs are same as Basic Doll pattern on page 20, use color **Cream 041**.

Head

Rnd 1: With two strands of **Fiesta pink 064** and 5 mm hook, ch 2, 6 sc in second chain from hook. (6)
Rnd 2: 2 sc in each st around. (12)
Rnd 3: (2 sc in next st, sc in next st) around. (18)
Rnd 4: (Sc in next 2 sts, 2 sc in next st) around. (24)
Rnd 5: (Sc in next 3 sts, 2 sc in next st) around. (30)
Rnd 6: Sc in next 2 sts, 2 sc in next st, (sc in next 4 sts, 2 sc in next st) 5 times, sc in next 2 sts. (36)
Rnd 7: (Sc in next 5 sts, 2 sc in next st) around. (42)
Rnd 8: Sc in each st around, changing to **Cream 041** in last 2 loops of st. (42)
Rnd 9: Working in back loops only. Sc in each st around. (42)
Rnd 10-13: Sc in each st around. (42)

Rnd 14: (Sc next 2 sts tog, sc in next 5 sts) around. (36)
Rnd 15: Sc in next 2 sts, sc next 2 sts tog, (sc in next 4 sts, sc next 2 sts tog) 5 times, sc in next 2 sts. (30)
Rnd 16: (Sc in next 3 sts, sc next 2 sts tog) around. (24)
Rnd 17: (Sc in next 2 sts, sc next 2 sts tog) around. (18)
Rnd 18: (Sc in next 4 sts, sc next 2 sts tog) around, join with sl st in first st, fasten off. (15)

Stuff head a little bit, insert safety eyes 7 sts apart between rnds 11-12 of head then stuff head more tightly.

With **Red embroidery thread** embroider mouth.

Hair

Working in rows. Rows 2-33 are working in back loops only.

Row 1: With 2 strands of **Fiesta pink 064** (hair color) and 5 mm hook, ch 10, sc in second chain from hook, sc in each ch across, turn. (9)
Row 2-32: Ch 1, sc in each st across, turn. (9)
Row 33: Ch 1, sc in each st across, leave long end for sewing, fasten off. (9)

Pin hair on head and sew to free loops of rnd 8.

Boy Doll

Materials

- DK, Light Worsted
  1. Hayfield Bonus DK Alpine 842 = 100 g
  2. Robin DK Brown 051 = 22 g
- 5 mm hook (US: H/8, UK: 6)
- DMC Pearl Cotton Thread Size 3 (115/3): Color Red 321 for embroider mouth
- One pair of 12mm safety eyes
- Tapestry needle
- Pins
- Polyester fibrefill = 135 g
- Stitch markers

Doll

Make one same as Basic Doll pattern on page 20. Use color **Alpine 842** for all Body parts.

Hair

Rnd 1: With 2 strands of **Brown 051** and 5 mm hook, ch 2, 6 sc in second chain from hook. (6)
Rnd 2: 2 sc in each st around. (12)
Rnd 3: (2 sc in next st, sc in next st) around. (18)
Rnd 4: (Sc in next 2 sts, 2 sc in next st) around. (24)
Rnd 5: (Sc in next 3 sts, 2 sc in next st) around. (30)
Rnd 6: Sc in next 2 sts, 2 sc in next st, (sc in next 4 sts, 2 sc in next st) 5 times, sc in next 2 sts. (36)
Rnd 7: (Sc in next 5 sts, 2 sc in next st) around. (42)
Rnd 8: Sc in next 3 sts, 2 sc in next st, (sc in next 6 sts, 2 sc in next st) 5 times, sc in next 3 sts. (48)
Rnd 9: Sc in each st around, turn.

Rows 10-17 are working in rows.
Row 10: Ch 1, sc in first st, sc in next 42 sts, sc next 2 sts tog, turn. (44)
Row 11: Ch 1, skip first st, sc in next 43 sts, turn. (43)
Row 12: Ch 1, sc in first st, sc in next 40 sts, skip next st, sc in next st, turn. (42)
Row 13: Ch 1, skip first st, sc in next 41 sts, turn. (41)
Row 14: Ch 1, sc in first st, sc in next 38 sts, skip next st, sc in next st, turn. (40)
Row 15: Ch 1, skip first st, (sc next 2 sts tog, sc in next 6 sts) 4 times, sc next 2 sts tog, sc in next 5 sts, turn. (34)
Row 16: Ch 1, sc in first st, sc in next 14 sts, sc next 2 sts tog, sc in next 15 sts, sc next 2 sts tog, turn. (32)
Row 17: Ch3 (count as one dc), dc next 3 sts tog, (dc next 2 sts tog, dc in next st) 8 times, dc next 4 sts tog, leave long end for sewing, fasten off. (19)

Put hair cap on head, pin it and sew to head. With **Brown 051** embroider hair as in pictures below.

Bear Doll

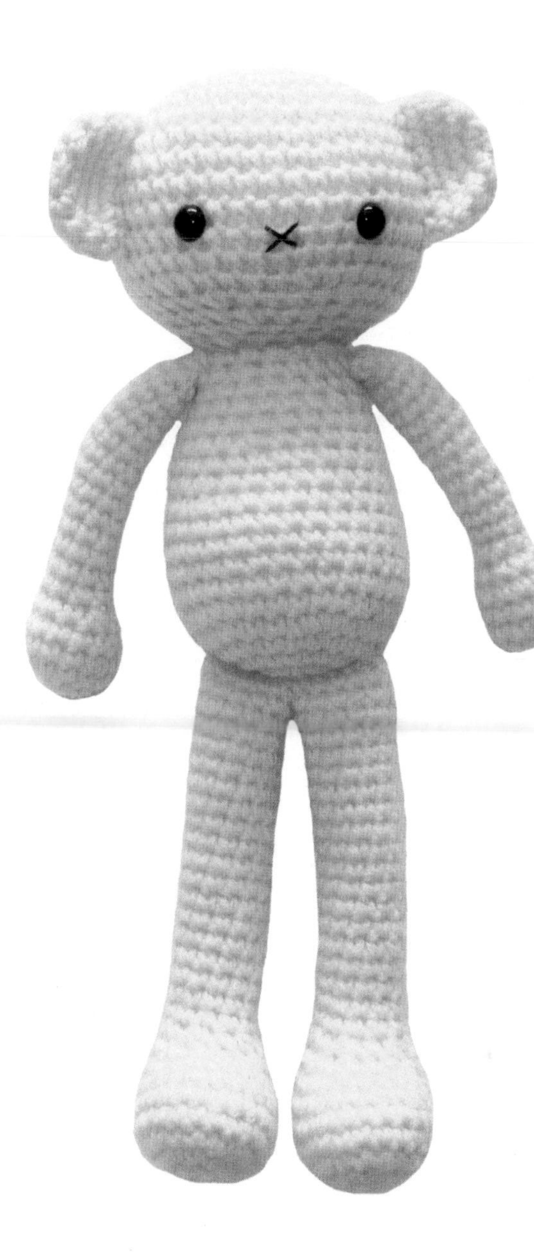

Materials

- DK, Light Worsted
  Robin DK: Pink 046 = 120 g
- 5 mm hook (US: H/8, UK: 6)
- DMC Pearl Cotton Thread Size 3 (115/3): Color Black 310 for embroider mouth
- One pair of 12mm safety eyes
- Tapestry needle
- Pins
- Polyester fibrefill = 135 g
- Stitch markers

Doll

Make one same as Basic Doll pattern on page 20. Use color **Pink 046** for all Body parts.

Bear Ear

Rnd 1: With two strands of **Pink 046** and 5 mm hook, ch 2, 6 sc in second chain from hook. (6)
Rnd 2: 2 sc in each st around. (12)
Rnd 3: (2 sc in next st, sc in next st) around. (18)
Rnd 4: Sc in each st around. (18)
Rnd 5: (Sc next 2 sts tog, sc in next 4 sts) around, sl st in first st, leave long end for sewing, fasten off. (15)

Sew the opening of the ears close. This makes it easier to sew them to the head. Pin ears to head before sewing them. This is very useful to keep them in the right position.

Sew the opening close.

Pin ears on rnds 7-12 of head and sew.

With **Black embroidery thread** embroider mouth (X).

Bunny Doll

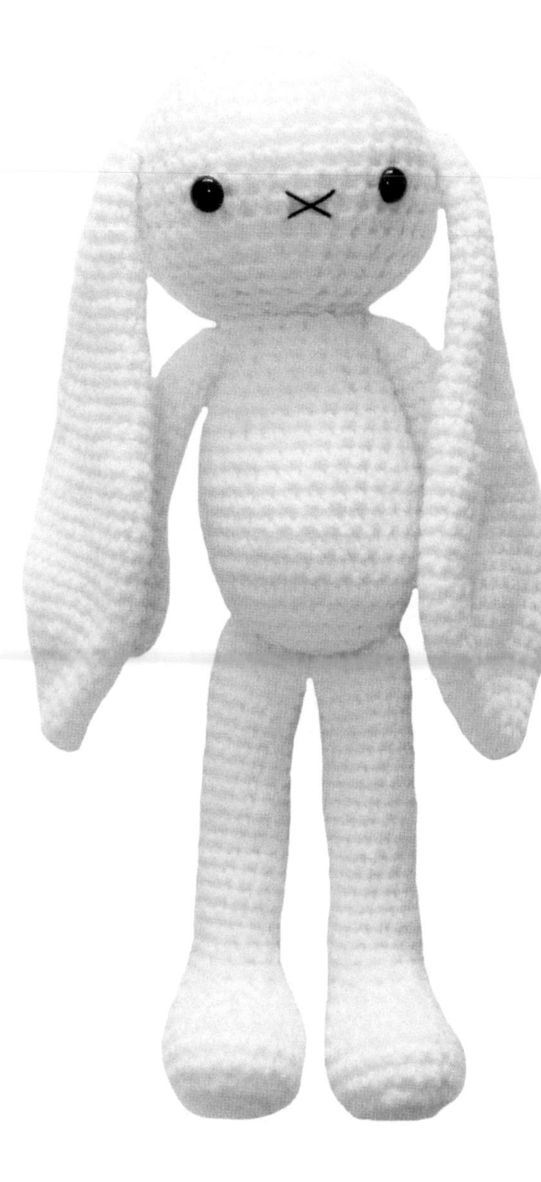

Materials

- DK, Light Worsted
  Robin DK: White 040 = 130 g
- 5 mm hook (US: H/8, UK: 6)
- DMC Pearl Cotton Thread Size 3 (115/3): Color Black 310 for embroider mouth
- One pair of 12mm safety eyes
- Tapestry needle
- Pins
- Polyester fibrefill = 135 g
- Stitch markers

Doll

Make one same as Basic Doll pattern on page 20. Use color **White 040** for all Body parts.

Ear

Rnd 1: With two strands of **White 040** and 5 mm hook, ch 2, 6 sc in second chain from hook. (6)
Rnd 2: (Sc in next st, 2 sc in next st) around. (9)
Rnd 3: (2 sc in next st, sc in next 2 sts) around. (12)
Rnd 4: (Sc in next 3 sts, 2 sc in next st) around. (15)
Rnd 5: Sc in next 2 sts, 2 sc in next st, (sc in next 4 sts, 2 sc in next st) 2 times, sc in next 2 sts. (18)
Rnd 6: (Sc in next 5 sts, 2 sc in next st) around. (21)
Rnd 7: Sc in next 3 sts, 2 sc in next st, (sc in next 6 sts, 2 sc in next st) 2 times, sc in next 3 sts. (24)
Rnd 8: (Sc in next 7 sts, 2 sc in next st) around. (27)
Rnd 9-15: Sc in each st around. (27)

Rnd 16: (Sc next 2 sts tog, sc in next 7 sts) around. (24)
Rnd 17-18: Sc in each st around. (24)
Rnd 19: Sc in next 3 sts, sc next 2 sts tog, (sc in next 6 sts, sc next 2 sts tog) 2 times, sc in next 3 sts. (21)
Rnd 20-21: Sc in each st around. (21)
Rnd 22: (Sc next 2 sts tog, sc in next 5 sts) around. (18)
Rnd 23-24: Sc in each st around. (18)
Rnd 25: Sc in next 2 sts, sc next 2 sts tog, (sc in next 4 sts, sc next 2 sts tog) 2 times, sc in next 2 sts. (15)
Rnd 26-27: Sc in each st around. (15)
Rnd 28: (Sc next 2 sts tog, sc in next 3 sts) around. (12)
Rnd 29-30: Sc in each st around. (12)
Rnd 31: (Sc next 2 sts tog, sc in next 2 sts) around. (9)
Rnd 32-33: Sc in each st around. (9)
Rnd 34: (Sc next 2 sts tog, sc in next st) around. (6)
Rnd 35: Sc in each st around, sl st in first st, leave long end for sewing, fasten off. (6)

Sew ears on rnds 9 of head. With **Black embroidery thread** embroider mouth (X).

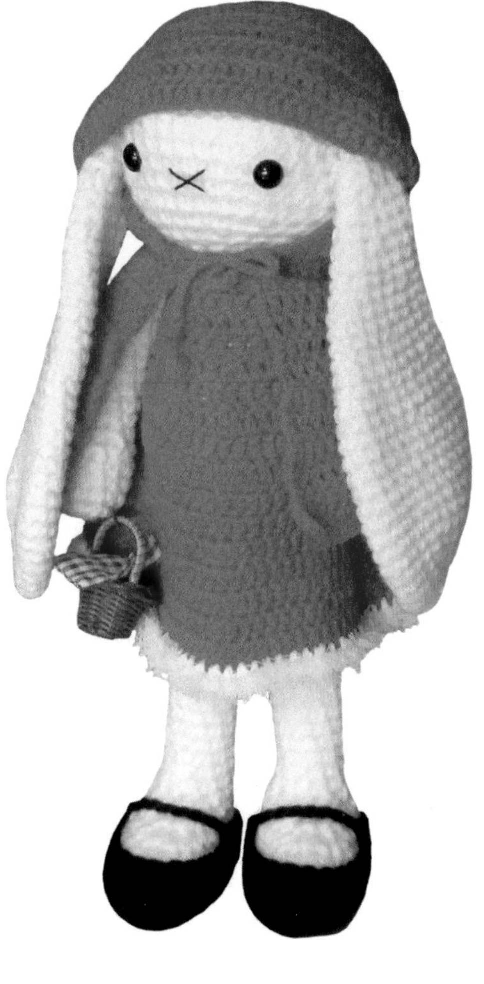

Underpants

Each Underpants uses 4 g of DK yarn (DK, Light Worsted).

Robin DK: White 040, Fondant 052, Pale Blue 047 and Pink 046

Underpants

Working in rows.

Row 1: With one strand of **Pink 046** and 4 mm hook, ch 20, sc in second chain from hook, sc in next 18 chs, turn. (19)
Row 2-4: Ch 1, sc in each st across, turn. (19)
Row 5: Ch 1, sc first 3 sts tog, sc in next 13 sts, sc next 3 sts tog, turn. (15)
Row 6: Ch 1, sc first 2 sts tog, sc in next 11 sts, sc next 2 sts tog, turn. (13)
Row 7: Ch 1, sc first 3 sts tog, sc in next 7 sts, sc in next 3 sts tog, turn. (9)
Row 8: Ch 1, sc first 2 sts tog, sc in next 5 sts, sc next 2 sts tog, turn. (7)
Row 9: Ch 1, sc first 3 sts tog, sc in next 1 sts, sc next 3 sts tog, turn. (3)
Row 10: Ch 1, sc 3 sts tog, turn. (1)
Row 11: Ch 1, 3 sc, turn. (3)
Row 12: Ch 1, 3 sc in first st, sc in next st, 3 sc in next st, turn. (7)
Row 13: Ch 1, 2 sc in first st, sc in next 5 sts, 2 sc in next st, turn. (9)
Row 14: Ch 1, 3 sc in first st, sc in next 7 sts, 3 sc in next st, turn. (13)
Row 15: Ch 1, 2 sc in first st, sc in next 11 sts, 2 sc in next st, turn. (15)
Row 16: Ch 1, 3 sc in first st, sc in next 13 sts, 3 sc in next st, turn. (19)
Row 17-19: Ch 1, sc in each st across, turn. (19)
Row 20: Ch 1, sc in each st across, leave long end for sewing, fasten off. (19)

Fold the underpants in half and sew on both sides (3 rows from top).

Bikini

One Bikini set uses 5 g of DK yarn (DK, Light Worsted).

Robin DK: Pale Blue 047, Turquoise 281, Pink 046 and Fondant 052.

Bikini Top

First Cup

Working in rows.

Row 1: With one strand of **Pink 046** and 4 mm hook, ch 15, sc in second chain from hook, sc in next 6 chs, turn. (7)

Row 2: Ch 1, sc first 2 sts tog, sc in next 3 sts, sc next 2 sts tog, turn. (5)

Row 3: Ch 1, sc first 2 sts tog, sc in next st, sc next 2 sts tog, turn. (3)

Row 4: Ch 1, sc in each st across, turn. (3)

Row 5: Ch 1, sc 3 sts tog, ch 30, fasten off.

The first cup made.

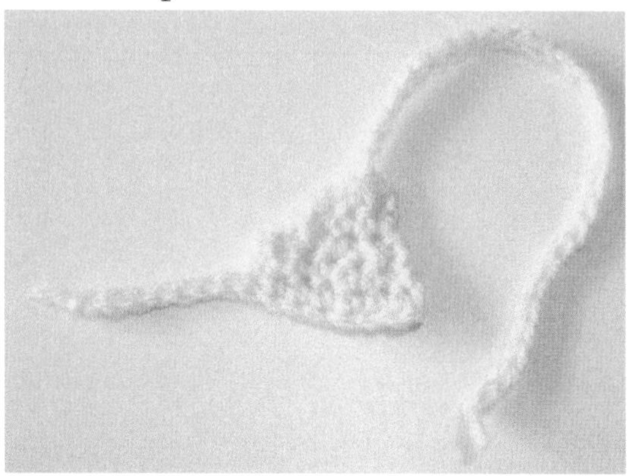

Second Cup

Working in rows.

Row 1: With one strand of **Pink 046** and 4 mm hook, join yarn in the ch next from the first cup, ch 1, sc in same st, sc in next 6 chs, turn. (7)

Row 2: Ch 1, sc first 2 sts tog, sc in next 3 sts, sc next 2 sts tog, turn. (5)

Row 3: Ch 1, sc first 2 sts tog, sc in next st, sc next 2 sts tog, turn. (3)

Row 4: Ch 1, sc in each st across, turn. (3)

Row 5: Ch 1, sc 3 sts tog, ch 30, fasten off.

String: to tie around the body

With one strand of **Fondant 052** and 4 mm hook, ch 30, sc in next 14 sts of bottom part of cups, ch 30, fasten off. (14 sts, 60 chs)

Bikini Bottom

Working in rows.

Row 1: With one strand of **Pink 046** and 4 mm hook, ch 20, sc in second chain from hook, sc in next 18 chs, turn. (19)
Row 2: Ch 1, sc in each st across, turn. (19)
Row 3: Ch 1, sc first 3 sts tog, sc in next 13 sts, sc next 3 sts tog, turn. (15)
Row 4: Ch 1, sc first 2 sts tog, sc in next 11 sts, sc next 2 sts tog, turn. (13)
Row 5: Ch 1, sc first 3 sts tog, sc in next 7 sts, sc in next 3 sts tog, turn. (9)
Row 6: Ch 1, sc first 2 sts tog, sc in next 5 sts, sc next 2 sts tog, turn. (7)
Row 7: Ch 1, sc first 3 sts tog, sc in next 1 sts, sc next 3 sts tog, turn. (3)
Row 8: Ch 1, sc 3 sts tog, turn. (1)
Row 9: Ch 1, 3 sc, turn. (3)
Row 10: Ch 1, 3 sc in first st, sc in next st, 3 sc in next st, turn. (7)
Row 11: Ch 1, 2 sc in first st, sc in next 5 sts, 2 sc in next st, turn. (9)
Row 12: Ch 1, 3 sc in first st, sc in next 7 sts, 3 sc in next st, turn. (13)
Row 13: Ch 1, 2 sc in first st, sc in next 11 sts, 2 sc in next st, turn. (15)
Row 14: Ch 1, 3 sc in first st, sc in next 13 sts, 3 sc in next st, turn. (19)
Row 15: Ch 1, sc in each st across, fasten off. (19)

String

Make strings for both sides of bikini.

With one strand of **Fondant 052** and 4 mm hook, ch 30, sc in next 19 sts of bikini, ch 30, fasten off. (19 sts, 60 chs)

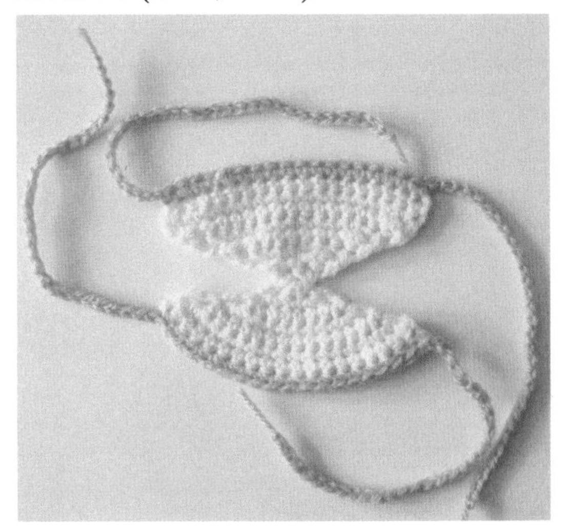

Swim Shorts

Swimming pants uses 10 g of DK yarn (DK, Light Worsted).

Robin DK: Spearmint 057 (8 g) and Turquoise 281 (2 g)

Swim Shorts

Rnd 1: With one strand of **Spearmint 057** and 4 mm hook, ch 40, sl st in first ch to form a ring, ch 3(count as one dc), dc in next 39 sts, join with sl st in first st, changing to color **Turquoise 281**. (40)

Rnd 2: Ch 1, sc in each st around, join with sl st in first st, changing to color **Spearmint**. (40)

Rnd 3: Ch 3(count as one dc), dc in next 39 sts, join with sl st in first st, changing to color **Turquoise**. (40)

Rnd 4: Ch 1, sc in each st around, join with sl st in first st, changing to **Spearmint**. (40)

Rnd 5: Ch 3(count as one dc), dc in next 39 sts, join with sl st in first st, changing to **Turquoise**. (40)

Rnd 6: Ch 1, sc in each st around, join with sl st in first st, changing to **Spearmint**. (40)

Rnd 7: Ch 3(count as one dc), dc in next 39 sts, join with sl st in first st, changing to **Turquoise**. (40)

Rnd 8: Start first leg; ch 1, sc in first st, sc in next 19 sts, skip next 20 sts, join with sl st in first st, changing to **Spearmint**. (20)

The picture shows after finished Rnd 8:

Rnd 9: Ch 3 (count as one dc), dc in next 19 sts, join with sl st in first st, changing to **Turquoise**. (20)
Rnd 10: Ch 1, sc in each st around, join with sl st in first st, changing to **Spearmint**. (20)
Rnd 11: Ch 3 (count as one dc), dc in next 19 sts, join with sl st in first st. (20)
Rnd 12: Ch 1, sc in each st around, join with sl st in first st, fasten off. (20)

Rnd 8: Start second leg; with one strand of **Turquoise** and 4 mm hook, join yarn to next free st on rnd 7, ch 1, sc in same st, sc in next 19 sts, join with sl st in first st, changing to **Spearmint**. (20)
Rnd 9: Ch 3 (count as one dc), dc in next 19 sts, join with sl st in first st, changing to **Turquoise**. (20)
Rnd 10: Ch 1, sc in each st around, join with sl st in first st, changing to **Spearmint**. (20)
Rnd 11: Ch 3 (count as one dc), dc in next 19 sts, join with sl st in first st. (20)
Rnd 12: Ch 1, sc in each st around, join with sl st in first st, fasten off. (20)

Sew the opening at crotch close.

Waist
Rnd 1: With one strand of **Turquoise 281** and 4 mm hook, join yarn to middle back of pants, ch 1, sc in each st around, join with sl st in first st. (40)
Rnd 2: Ch 1, sc in each st around, join with sl st in first st, fasten off. (40)

Boots

One pair of Boots use 28 g of DK yarn (DK, Light Worsted).

Robin DK: Brown 051, Blue Madonna 033

Trim: use 2 g (for one pair) of Chunky yarn.

5
Bulky

Schachenmayr Nomotta Cassiopeia, color: White

Boots

Make 2.

Rnd 1: With 2 strands of **Brown 051** and 5 mm hook, ch 9, sc in second chain from hook, sc in next 6 chs, 3 sc in last ch; working in remaining loops on opposite side of chain, sc in next 6 chs, 2 sc in next ch. (18)

```
  X X X X X X X X O
X O O O O O O O O X
  X X X X X X X X
```

o = chain x = sc

Rnd 2: 2 sc in next st, sc in next 6 sts, 2 sc in next 3 sts, sc in next 6 sts, 2 sc in next 2 sts. (24)

Rnd 3: Sc in next st, 2 sc in next st, sc in next 7 sts, 2 sc in next st, (sc in next st, 2 sc in next st) 2 times, sc in next 7 sts, 2 sc in next st, sc in next st, 2 sc in next st. (30)

Rnd 4-7: Sc in each st around. (30)

Rnd 8: Sc in next 10 sts, sc next 2 sts tog, (sc in next st, sc next 2 sts tog) 2 times, sc in next 12 sts. (27)

Rnd 9: Sc in next 10 sts, (sc next 2 sts tog) 3 times, sc in next 11 sts. (24)

Rnd 10: Sc in next 7 sts, (sc next 2 sts tog) 2 times, sc in next st, (sc next 2 sts tog) 2 times, sc in next 8 sts. (20)

Rnd 11: Sc in next 7 sts, sc next 2 sts tog, sc in next st, sc next 2 sts tog, sc in next 8 sts. (18)

Rnd 12: Sc in each st around. (18)

Rnd 13: Sc in each st around, changing to **Cassiopeia color White** (one strand) in last 2 loops of last st. (18)

Rnd 14: Sc in each st around.

Rnd 15: Sc in each st around, sl st in first st, fasten off.

Slippers

One pair uses 14 g of DK yarn (DK, Light Worsted).
Robin DK: Red 042, Blue Madonna 033, Turquoise 281, Acid Yellow 060

Trim: use 2 g (for one pair) of Chunky yarn
Schachenmayr Nomotta Cassiopeia, color: White

Slippers

Make 2.
Rnd 1: With 2 strands of **Red 042** and 5 mm hook, ch 2, 7 sc in second chain from hook. (7)
Rnd 2: 2 sc in each st around. (14)
Rnd 3: (Sc in next st, 2 sc in next st) around. (21)
Rnd 4-8: Sc in each st around. (21)

Working in rows.
Row 9: Sc in next 10 sts, turn. (10)
Row 10: Ch 1, sc in next 10 sts, turn. (10)
Row 11: Ch 1, sc first 2 sts tog, sc in next 6 sts, sc next 2 sts tog, turn. (8)
Row 12: Ch 1, sc first 2 sts tog, sc in next 4 sts, sc next 2 sts tog, turn. (6)
Row 13: Ch 1, sc first 2 sts tog, sc in next 2 sts, sc next 2 sts tog, turn. (4)
Row 14: Ch 1, sc in each st around the edge of slipper, fasten off.

Slippers with white trim:
Row 13: Ch 1, sc first 2 sts tog, sc in next 2 sts, sc next 2 sts tog, changing to **Cassiopeia color White** (one strand), turn. (4)
Row 14: Ch 1, sc in each st around the edge of slipper, fasten off.

Mary Jane Shoes

Mary Jane Shoes

One Pair uses 15 g of DK yarn (DK, Light Worsted)

Robin DK: Turquoise 281, Jaffa(orange) 063 and Pink 046

Two 25 mm Flower Buttons for one pair.

Make 2.

Rnd 1: With 2 strands of **Pink 046** and 5 mm hook, ch 9, sc in second chain from hook, sc in next 6 chs, 3 sc in last ch; working in remaining loops on opposite side of chain, sc in next 6 chs, 2 sc in next ch. (18)

```
  X X X X X X X X O
X O O O O O O O O X
  X X X X X X X X
```

o = chain x = sc

Rnd 2: 2 sc in next st, sc in next 6 sts, 2 sc in next 3 sts, sc in next 6 sts, 2 sc in next 2 sts. (24)

Rnd 3: Sc in next st, 2 sc in next st, sc in next 7 sts, 2 sc in next st, (sc in next st, 2 sc in next st) 2 times, sc in next 7 sts, 2 sc in next st, sc in next st, 2 sc in next st. (30)

Rnd 4-6: Sc in each st around. (30)

Rnd 7: Sc in next 10 sts, sc next 2 sts tog, (sc in next st, sc next 2 sts tog) 2 times, sc in next 12 sts. (27)

Rnd 8: Sc in next 6 sts, ch 8, skip 14 sts, sc in next 7 sts, fasten off.

Sew buttons on outer side of both shoes.

Ballet Pumps

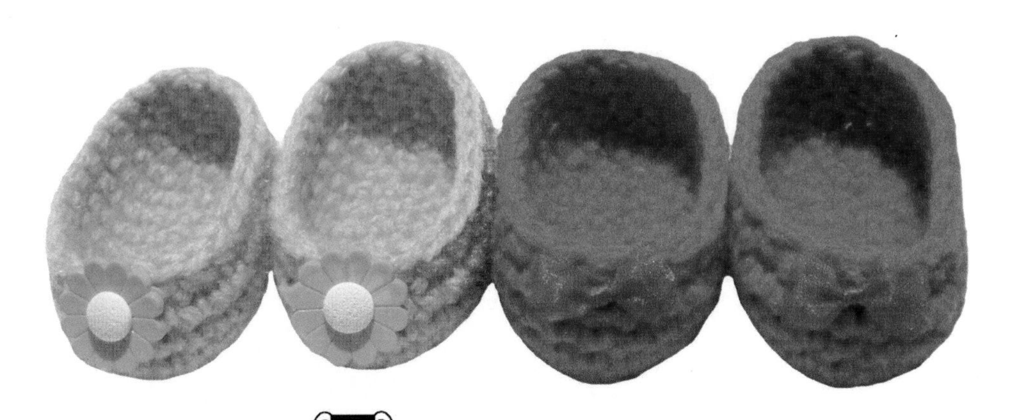

One Pair uses 15 g of DK yarn (DK, Light Worsted)

3 Light

Robin DK: Red 042 and Aqua 130

Two 25 mm Flower Buttons for one pair.
Two Red Bows for one pair.

Ballet Pumps

Make 2.

Rnd 1- 6: Same as Mary Jane Shoes.

Rnd 7: Sc in next 10 sts, sc next 2 sts tog, (sc in next st, sc next 2 sts tog) 2 times, sc in next 10 sts, sc next 2 sts tog, fasten off. (26)

Sew buttons or bows on shoes.

Trainers

One Pair uses 20 g of DK yarn (DK, Light Worsted)
Robin DK: Royal(blue) 086, Black 044 and a little bit of White 040 to embroider a white line on the shoes.

Trainers

Make 2.

Rnd 1: With 2 strands of **Royal 086** and 5 mm hook, ch 9, sc in second chain from hook, sc in next 6 chs, 3 sc in last ch; working in remaining loops on opposite side of chain, sc in next 6 chs, 2 sc in next ch. (18)

```
    X X X X X X X X O
  X O O O O O O O O X
    X X X X X X X X
```

o = chain x = sc

Rnd 2: 2 sc in next st, sc in next 6 sts, 2 sc in next 3 sts, sc in next 6 sts, 2 sc in next 2 sts. (24)
Rnd 3: Sc in next st, 2 sc in next st, sc in next 7 sts, 2 sc in next st, (sc in next st, 2 sc in next st) 2 times, sc in next 7 sts, 2 sc in next st, sc in next st, 2 sc in next st. (30)
Rnd 4-7: Sc in each st around. (30)
Rnd 8: Sc in next 10 sts, sc next 2 sts tog, (sc in next st, sc next 2 sts tog) 2 times, sc in next 12 sts. (27)
Rnd 9: Sc in next 10 sts, (sc next 2 sts tog) 3 times, sc in next 11 sts. (24)
Rnd 10: Sc in next 7 sts, (sc next 2 sts tog) 2 times, sc in next st, (sc next 2 sts tog) 2 times, sc in next 8 sts. (20)
Rnd 11: Sc in each st around, sl st in first st, fasten off.

Blue shoes: With **White 040** embroider white line on shoes.

Christmas Hat

One hat uses 35 g of DK yarn (DK, Light Worsted).
Robin DK: Pale Blue 047 and Red 042

Trim: use 15 g (one hat) of Chunky yarn.

Schachenmayr nomotta Cassiopeia, color: White

Knit Pro Pom Pom maker size 5.5 cm (2.2")
Robin DK: White 040 = 10 g (one Pom Pom)

Christmas Hat

Rnd 1: With two strands of **Red 042** and 5 mm hook, ch 2, 6 sc in second chain from hook. (6)
Rnd 2: Sc in each st around. (6)
Rnd 3: (2 sc in next st, sc in next st) around. (9)
Rnd 4: Sc in each st around. (9)
Rnd 5: (Sc in next 2 sts, 2 sc in next st) around. (12)
Rnd 6: Sc in each st around. (12)
Rnd 7: (2 sc in next st, sc in next 3 sts) around. (15)
Rnd 8: Sc in each st around. (15)

Rnd 9: Sc in next 2 sts, 2 sc in next st, (sc in next 4 sts, 2 sc in next st) 2 times, sc in next 2 sts. (18)
Rnd 10: Sc in each st around. (18)
Rnd 11: (2 sc in next st, sc in next 5 sts) around. (21)
Rnd 12: Sc in each st around. (21)
Rnd 13: Sc in next 3 sts, 2 sc in next st, (sc in next 6 sts, 2 sc in next st) 2 times, sc in next 3 sts. (24)
Rnd 14: Sc in each st around. (24)
Rnd 15: (2 sc in next st, sc in next 7sts) around. (27)
Rnd 16: Sc in each st around. (27)
Rnd 17: Sc in next 4 sts, 2 sc in next st, (sc in next 8 sts, 2 sc in next st) 2 times, sc in next 4 sts. (30)
Rnd 18: Sc in each st around. (30)
Rnd 19: (2 sc in next st, sc in next 9 sts) around. (33)
Rnd 20: Sc in each st around. (33)
Rnd 21: Sc in next 5 sts, 2 sc in next st, (sc in next 10 sts, 2 sc in next st) 2 times, sc in next 5 sts. (36)
Rnd 22: Sc in each st around. (36)
Rnd 23: (2 sc in next st, sc in next 11 sts) around. (39)
Rnd 24: Sc in each st around. (39)
Rnd 25: Sc in next 6 sts, 2 sc in next st, (sc in next 12 sts, 2 sc in next st) 2 times, sc in next 6 sts. (42)
Rnd 26: Sc in each st around. (42)
Rnd 27: (2 sc in next st, sc in next 13 sts) around. (45)
Rnd 28: Sc in each st around. (45)
Rnd 29: Sc in next 7 sts, 2 sc in next st, (sc in next 14 sts, 2 sc in next st) 2 times, sc in next 7 sts. (48)
Rnd 30: Sc in each st around. (48)
Rnd 31: (2 sc in next st, sc in next 15 sts) around. (51)
Rnd 32: Sc in each st around. (51)
Rnd 33: Sc in next 8 sts, 2 sc in next st, (sc in next 16 sts, 2 sc in next st) 2 times, sc in next 8 sts. (54)
Rnd 34: Sc in each st around, changing to **Cassiopeia color White** (one strand) in last 2 loops of last st. (54)
Rnd 35-37: Sc in each st around. (54)
Rnd 38: Sc in each st around, join with sl st in first st, fasten off. (54)

Pom Pom With **White 040**, make one Pom Pom size 2.2" (5.5 cm), attach it on top of Christmas Hat.

Sleeping Hat

One hat uses 36 g of DK yarn (DK, Light Worsted). 3 Light

Red Hat: Robin DK: Red 042 = 4 g and Robin Paintbox DK color Tropics 1113 = 32 g

Blue Hat: Robin DK: Pale Blue 047 = 20 g and Blue Madonna 033 = 16 g

Knit Pro Pom Pom maker size 3.5 cm (1.4")
One Pom Pom uses 5 g of DK yarn
Robin DK: Pale Blue 047 and Red 042

Sleeping Hat

Rnd 1: With one strand of **Tropics 1113** and 4 mm hook, ch 4, 5 dc in 4th chain from hook, join with sl st in first st. (6)
Rnd 2: Ch 3 (count as one dc), 2 dc in next st, (dc in next st, 2 dc in next st) 2 times, join with sl st in first st. (9)
Rnd 3: Ch 3, dc in each st around, join with sl st in first st. (9)
Rnd 4: Ch 3, dc in next st, 2 dc in next st, (dc in next 2 sts, 2 dc in next st) 2 times, join with sl st in first st. (12)
Rnd 5: Ch 3, dc in each st around, join with sl st in first st. (12)

Rnd 6: Ch 3, dc in next 2 sts, 2 dc in next st, (dc in next 3 sts, 2 dc in next st) 2 times, join with sl st in first st. (15)
Rnd 7: Ch 3, dc in each st around, join with sl st in first st. (15)
Rnd 8: Ch 3, dc in next st, 2 dc in next st, (dc in next 4 sts, 2 dc in next st) 2 times, dc in next 2 sts, join with sl st in first st. (18)
Rnd 9: Ch 3, dc in each st around, join with sl st in first st. (18)
Rnd 10: Ch 3, dc in next 4 sts, 2 dc in next st, (dc in next 5 sts, 2 dc in next st) 2 times, join with sl st in first st. (21)
Rnd 11: Ch 3, dc in each st around, join with sl st in first st. (21)
Rnd 12: Ch 3, dc in next 2 sts, 2 dc in next st, (dc in next 6 sts, 2 dc in next st) 2 times, dc in next 3 sts, join with sl st in first st. (24)
Rnd 13: Ch 3, dc in each st around, join with sl st in first st. (24)
Rnd 14: Ch 3, dc in next 6 sts, 2 dc in next st, (dc in next 7 sts, 2 dc in next st) 2 times, join with sl st in first st. (27)
Rnd 15: Ch 3, dc in each st around, join with sl st in first st. (27)
Rnd 16: Ch 3, dc in next 3 sts, 2 dc in next st, (dc in next 8 sts, 2 dc in next st) 2 times, dc in next 4 sts, join with sl st in first st. (30)
Rnd 17: Ch 3, dc in each st around, join with sl st in first st. (30)
Rnd 18: Ch 3, dc in next 8 sts, 2 dc in next st, (dc in next 9 sts, 2 dc in next st) 2 times, join with sl st in first st. (33)
Rnd 19: Ch 3, dc in each st around, join with sl st in first st. (33)
Rnd 20: Ch 3, dc in next 4 sts, 2 dc in next st, (dc in next 10 sts, 2 dc in next st) 2 times, dc in next 5 sts, join with sl st in first st. (36)
Rnd 21: Ch 3, dc in each st around, join with sl st in first st. (36)
Rnd 22: Ch 3, dc in next 10 sts, 2 dc in next st, (dc in next 11 sts, 2 dc in next st) 2 times, join with sl st in first st. (39)
Rnd 23: Ch 3, dc in each st around, join with sl st in first st. (39)
Rnd 24: Ch 3, dc in next 5 sts, 2 dc in next st, (dc in next 12 sts, 2 dc in next st) 2 times, dc in next 6 sts, join with sl st in first st. (42)
Rnd 25: Ch 3, dc in each st around, join with sl st in first st. (42)
Rnd 26: Ch 3, dc in next 12 sts, 2 dc in next st, (dc in next 13 sts, 2 dc in next st) 2 times, join with sl st in first st. (45)
Rnd 27: Ch 3, dc in each st around, join with sl st in first st. (45)
Rnd 28: Ch 3, dc in next 6 sts, 2 dc in next st, (dc in next 14 sts, 2 dc in next st) 2 times, dc in next 7 sts, join with sl st in first st. (48)
Rnd 29: Ch 3, dc in each st around, join with sl st in first st. (48)
Rnd 30: Ch 3, dc in next 14 sts, 2 dc in next st, (dc in next 15 sts, 2 dc in next st) 2 times, join with sl st in first st. (51)
Rnd 31: Ch 3, dc in each st around, join with sl st in first st. (51)
Rnd 32: Ch 3, dc in next 7 sts, 2 dc in next st, (dc in next 16 sts, 2 dc in next st) 2 times, dc in next 8 sts, join with sl st in first st. (54)
Rnd 33: Ch 3, dc in each st around, join with sl st in first st. (54)
Rnd 34: Ch 3, dc in next 16 sts, 2 dc in next st, (dc in next 17 sts, 2 dc in next st) 2 times, join with sl st in first st. (57)
Rnd 35: Ch 3, dc in next 8 sts, 2 dc in next st, (dc in next 18 sts, 2 dc in next st) 2 times, dc in next 9 sts, join with sl st in first st. (60)
Rnd 36: Ch 3, dc in next 18 sts, 2 dc in next st, (dc in next 19 sts, 2 dc in next st) 2 times, join with sl st in first st, changing to **Red 042** (one strand). (63)
Rnd 37: Ch 3, dc in next 9 sts, 2 dc in next st, (dc in next 20 sts, 2 dc in next st) 2 times, dc in next 10 sts, join with sl st in first st. (66)
Rnd 38: Ch 1, sl st in each st around, fasten off. (66)

Pom Pom With **Red 042**, make one Pom Pom size 3.5 cm (1.4"), attach it on top of the Sleeping Hat.

Blue Sleeping Hat
Color **Pale Blue 047**: Rnds 1,3,5,7,9,11,...,37,38
Color **Blue Madonna 033**: Rnds 2,4,6,8,...,36
With **Pale Blue 047**, make Pom Pom size 3.5 cm (1.4").

Sun Hat

One Hat uses 35 g of DK yarn (DK, Light Worsted)

Robin DK color Fondant 052

Sun Hat

Rnd 1: With two strands of **Fondant 052** and 5 mm hook, ch 2, 6 sc in second chain from hook. (6)
Rnd 2: 2 sc in each st around. (12)
Rnd 3: (2 sc in next st, sc in next st) around. (18)
Rnd 4: (Sc in next 2 sts, 2 sc in next st) around. (24)
Rnd 5: (Sc in next 3 sts, 2 sc in next st) around. (30)
Rnd 6: Sc in next 2 sts, 2 sc in next st, (sc in next 4 sts, 2 sc in next st) 5 times, sc in next 2 sts. (36)
Rnd 7: (Sc in next 5 sts, 2 sc in next st) around. (42)
Rnd 8: Sc in next 3 sts, 2 sc in next st, (sc in next 6 sts, 2 sc in next st) 5 times, sc in next 3 sts. (48)
Rnd 9-17: Sc in each st around. (48)
Rnd 18: Working in front loops only. (2 sc in next st, sc in next 2 sts) around. (64)
Rnd 19: (Sc in next 7 sts, 2 sc in next st) around. (72)
Rnd 20: Sc in next 4 sts, 2 sc in next st, (sc in next 8 sts, 2 sc in next st) 5 times, sc in next 4 sts. (80)
Rnd 21: Sc in each st around, sl st in first st, fasten off. (80)

Decorate the hat as you wish.

Cap

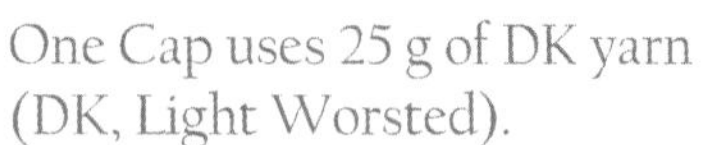
One Cap uses 25 g of DK yarn

(DK, Light Worsted).

Robin DK color Royal 086

Cap

Rnd 1: With two strands of **Royal 086** and 5 mm hook, ch 2, 6 sc in second chain from hook. (6)
Rnd 2: 2 sc in each st around. (12)
Rnd 3: (2 sc in next st, sc in next st) around. (18)
Rnd 4: (Sc in next 2 sts, 2 sc in next st) around. (24)
Rnd 5: (Sc in next 3 sts, 2 sc in next st) around. (30)
Rnd 6: Sc in next 2 sts, 2 sc in next st, (sc in next 4 sts, 2 sc in next st) 5 times, sc in next 2 sts. (36)
Rnd 7: (Sc in next 5 sts, 2 sc in next st) around. (42)
Rnd 8: Sc in next 3 sts, 2 sc in next st, (sc in next 6 sts, 2 sc in next st) 5 times, sc in next 3 sts. (48)
Rnd 9-15: Sc in each st around. (48)

Rows 16-20 are working in rows.

Row 16: Starting of Visor, working in front loops only, sc next 2 sts tog, (sc in next 2 sts, 2 sc in next st) 4 times, sc in next 2 sts, sc next 2 sts tog, turn. (20)
Row 17: Ch 1, sc first 2 sts tog, sc in next 16 sts, sc next 2 sts tog, turn. (18)
Row 18: Ch 1, sc first 2 sts tog, sc in next 14 sts, sc next 2 sts tog, turn. (16)
Row 19: Ch 1, sc first 2 sts tog, sc in next 12 sts, sc next 2 sts tog, turn. (14)
Row 20: Ch 1, sc first 2 sts tog, sc in next 10 sts, sc next 2 sts tog, fasten off. (12)

Pyjamas

One Pyjamas uses 25 g of DK yarn (DK, Light Worsted).

Robin Paintbox DK color Tropics 1113 and Robin DK color Pale Blue 047

Pyjamas

Working in rows.

Row 1: With one strand of **Tropics 1113** and 4 mm hook, ch 80, dc in 4th chain from hook, dc in next 76 chs, turn. (78)

Rows 2-6 are working in back loops only.

Row 2-6: Ch 3 (count as one dc), dc in each st across, turn. (78)

Row 7: Ch 1, sc in same st, sc in next 29 sts, ch 18, skip 18 sts, sc in next 30 sts, turn. (60 sts, 18 chs)

Row 8: Ch 3 (count as one dc), dc in next 29 sts, dc in next 18 chs, dc in next 30 sts, turn. (78)

Rows 9-13 are working in back loops only.

Row 9-12: Ch 3, dc in each st across, turn. (78)

Row 13: Ch 3, dc in each st across, leave long end for sewing, fasten off. (78)

Size before folding: 15.6 x 4.8 inches (39 x 12 cm).

Fold pyjama and sew 2 pieces together and leave 2 inches/ 5 cm for arm hole.

Sun Dress

3 Light

One Dress uses 30 g of DK yarn (DK, Light Worsted).
Robin DK: Pale Blue 047 = 5 g and Turquoise 281 = 25 g

One 5 mm Snap Fastener.

Dress

Working in rows.

Row 1: With one strand of **Pale Blue 047** and 4 mm hook, ch 46, sc in second chain from hook, sc in next 44 chs, turn. (45)

Row 2: Ch 1, sc in first st, sc in next 7 sts, ch 6, skip 10 sts, sc in next 9 sts, ch 6, skip 10 sts, sc in next 8 sts, turn. (25 sts, 12 chs)

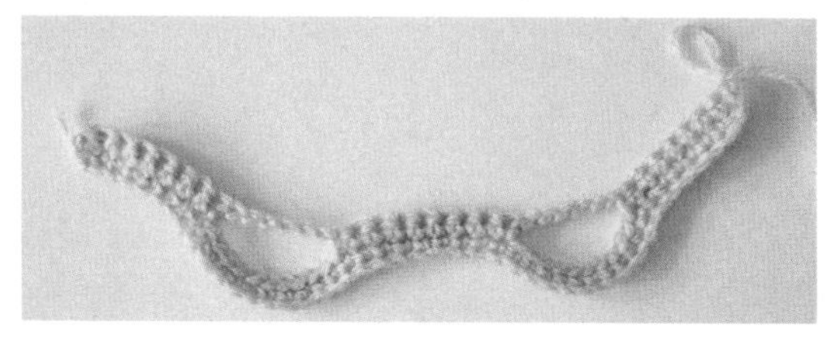

Row 3: Ch 1, sc in first st, sc in next 7 sts, sc in next 6 chs, sc in next 9 sts, sc in next 6 chs, sc in next 8 sts, turn. (37)

Row 4: Ch 1, sc in each st across, turn. (37)

Row 5: Ch 1, sc first st, sc in next 4 sts, 2 sc in next st, (sc in next 10 sts, 2 sc in next st) 2 times, sc in next 5 sts, 2 sc in next st, sc in next 3 sts, turn. (41)

Rnds 6 - 22 are working in rounds and join with sl st at the end of round.

Rnd 6: Ch 1, sc in first st, sc in next 38 sts, skip last 2 sts, join with sl st in first st. (39)

Rnd 7: Ch 1, sc in first st, sc in next 38 sts, join with sl st in first st. (39)
Rnd 8: Ch 1, sc in first st, sc in next 11 sts, 2 sc in next st, (sc in next 12 sts, 2 sc in next st) 2 times, changing to **Turquoise 281** in last 2 loops of last st, join with sl st in first st. (42)
Rnd 9: Ch 3 (count as one dc), 2 dc in same st, skip next st, (3 dc in next st, skip next st) 20 times, sl st in first st.

Rnd 10-21: Ch 3 (count as one dc), 2 dc in same space, 3 dc in next space around, sl st in first st.
Rnd 22: Ch 1, sc in same space, ch 2, 2 dc in same space, (sc in next space, ch 2, 2 dc in same space) 20 times, sl st in first st, fasten off.

Sew snap fasteners on dress (mark X), see picture.

Dungarees Dress

One Dress uses 25 g of DK yarn (DK, Light Worsted).
Robin DK color Aqua 130 = 25 g

Two 12 mm heart buttons.

Dungarees Dress

Rnd 1: With one strand of **Aqua 130** and 4 mm hook, ch 50, sl st in first ch to form a ring, ch 3 (count as one dc), dc in next 49 chs, join with sl st in first st. (50)
Rnd 2-6: Ch 3(count as one dc), dc in next 49 sts, join with sl st in first st. (50)
Rnd 7: Ch 3(count as one dc), dc in next 8 sts, 2 dc in next st, (dc in next 9 sts, 2 dc in next st) 4 times, join with sl st in first st. (55)
Rnd 8: Ch 3(count as one dc), dc in each st around, join with sl st in first st. (55)
Rnd 9: Ch 3(count as one dc), dc in next 4 sts, 2 dc in next st, (dc in next 10 sts, 2 dc in next st) 4 times, dc in next 5 sts, join with sl st in first st. (60)
Rnd 10: Ch 3(count as one dc), dc in each st around, join with sl st in first st. (60)
Rnd 11: Ch 3(count as one dc), dc in next 10 sts, 2 dc in next st, (dc in next 11 sts, 2 dc in next st) 4 times, join with sl st in first st. (65)
Rnd 12: Ch 3(count as one dc), dc in each st around, join with sl st in first st. (65)
Rnd 13: Ch 3(count as one dc), dc in each st around, join with sl st in first st, fasten off. (65)

Dungarees Dress & Dungarees: the buttons go in between the dc stitches on row 3 of bib.

Bib

Working in rows.

Row 1: With one strand of **Aqua 130** and 4 mm hook, join yarn to the 7th stitch from the edge, ch 3 (count as one dc), dc in next 12 sts, turn. (13)

Row 2: Ch 3 (count as one dc), dc in next 12 sts, turn. (13)

Row 3: Ch 3 (count as one dc), dc in next 12 sts; working around the edge of dress, ch 1, sc around the edge, join with sl st in first st, fasten off.

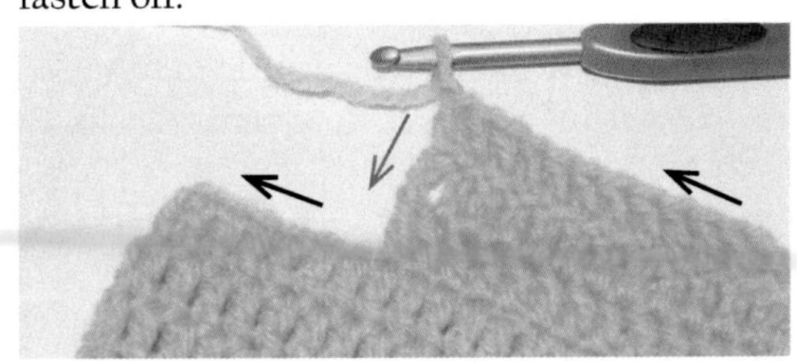

Strap

Make 2.

Row 1: With one strand of **Aqua 130** and 4 mm hook, ch 30, sc in second chain from hook, sc in next 28 chs, leave long end for sewing, fasten off. (29)

Sew straps to the back as in picture.

Cross the straps and sew in the middle (mark X).

Sew buttons on straps.

Dungarees

One Dungarees uses 25 g of DK yarn (DK, Light Worsted).

Robin DK: Turquoise 281

Two 12 mm buttons for one Dungarees.

Dungarees

Rnd 1: With one strand of **Turquoise 281** and 4 mm hook, ch 50, sl st in first ch to form a ring, ch 3 (count as one dc), dc in next 49 chs, join with sl st in first st. (50)

Rnd 2-8: Ch 3(count as one dc), dc in next 49 chs, join with sl st in first st. (50)

Rnd 9: Start first leg; ch 3 (count as one dc), dc in next 24 sts, skip next 25 sts, join with sl st in first st. (25)

Rnd 10-12: Ch 3 (count as one dc), dc in next 24 sts, join with sl st in first st. (25)

Rnd 13: Ch 3 (count as one dc), dc in next 24 sts, join with sl st in first st, fasten off. (25)

Rnd 9: Start second leg; With one strand of **Turquoise 281** and 4 mm hook, join yarn to next free st on rnd 8, ch 3 (count as one dc), dc in next 24 sts, join with sl st in first st. (25)

Rnd 10-12: Ch 3 (count as one dc), dc in next 24 sts, join with sl st in first st. (25)

Rnd 13: Ch 3 (count as one dc), dc in next 24 sts, join with sl st in first st, fasten off. (25)

Sew the opening at crotch close.

Bib

Making in rows.

Row 1: With one strand of **Turquoise 281** and 4 mm hook, join yarn to the 7th stitch from the edge, ch 3 (count as one dc), dc in next 12 sts, turn. (13)

Rnd 2: Ch 3 (count as one dc), dc in next 12 sts, turn. (13)

Rnd 3: Ch 3 (count as one dc), dc in next 12 sts; working around the edge of dungarees, ch 1, sc around the edge, join with sl st in first st, fasten off.

Strap

Make 2.

Row 1: With one strand of **Turquoise 281** and 4 mm hook, ch 30, sc in second chain from hook, sc in next 28 chs, leave long end for sewing, fasten off. (29)

Sew straps to the back as in picture.

Cross the straps and sew in the middle (mark X). Sew buttons on straps.

Christmas Dress

One dress uses 25 g of DK yarn (DK, Light Worsted). 3 Light
Robin DK: Pale Blue 047 and Red 042.

Trim: use 5 g (one dress) of Chunky 5 Bulky
Schachenmayr nomotta Cassiopeia, color: White.

Three 5 mm Snap Fasteners for one dress.

Dress

Top part

Working in rows.

Row 1: With one strand of **Red 042** and 4 mm hook, ch 50, dc in 4th chain from hook, dc in next 46 chs, turn. (48)

Row 2: Ch 3 (count as one dc), dc in each st across, turn. (48)

Row 3: Ch 3, dc in next 2 sts, dc next 2 sts tog, (dc in next 6 sts, dc next 2 sts tog) 5 times, dc in next 3 sts, turn. (42)

Row 4: Ch 3, dc in next 4 sts, dc next 2 sts tog, (dc in next 5 sts, dc next 2 sts tog) 5 times, turn. (36)

Row 5: Ch 3, dc in next st, dc next 2 sts tog, (dc in next 4 sts, dc next 2 sts tog) 5 times, dc in next 2 sts, turn. (30)

Row 6-7: Ch 3, dc in each st across, turn. (30)

Row 8: Ch 3, dc in next 7 sts, ch 10, dc in next 13 sts, ch 10, dc in next 9 sts, turn. (30 dc, 20 ch)

Row 9: Ch 3, dc in next 8 sts, (dc next 2 chs tog) 5 times, dc in next 13 sts, (dc next 2 chs tog) 5 times, dc in next 8 sts. (40)

Edge of top: Working in end of rows 1-9.
Row 1: Ch 1, 2 sc in end of row 9, 2 sc in next end of 8 rows, turn. (18)

Row 2: Ch 1, sc in each st across, fasten off. (18)

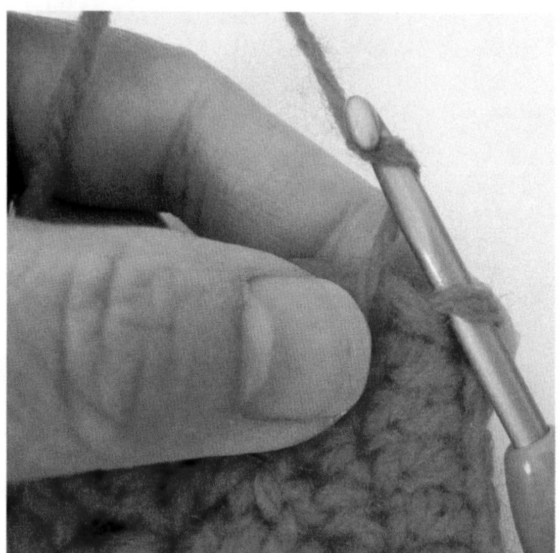

Edge of top on the other side:
Working in end of rows 1-9.
Row 1: With one strand of **Red 042** and 4 mm hook, join at the end of row 1, ch 1, 2 sc in end of row 1, 2 sc in next end of 8 rows, turn. (18)

Row 2: Ch 1, sc in each st across, do not fasten off. (18)

Picture shows finished row 2.

Skirt: Working in rounds and join with sl st at the end of round.

Rnd 1: Ch 1, sc in end of row 2 of edge of top, sc in end of next row; working in starting chain of top, sc in next 48 chs, skip 2 rows (edge of top), join with sl st in first st. (50)

Picture shows the first 4 sts of round 1.

Picture shows the end of round 1, after finished 50 sts, 2 rows marked blue which have to be skipped.

Rnd 2: Ch 3 (count as one dc), dc in next 49 sts, join with sl st in first st. (50)
Rnd 3: Ch 3, dc in next 8 sts, 2 dc in next st, (dc in next 9 sts, 2 dc in next st) 4 times, join with sl st in first st. (55)
Rnd 4: Ch 3, dc in next 4 sts, 2 dc in next st, (dc in next 10 sts, 2 dc in next st) 4 times, dc in next 5 sts, join with sl st in first st. (60)
Rnd 5: Ch 3, dc in next 10 sts, 2 dc in next st, (dc in next 11 sts, 2 dc in next st) 4 times, join with sl st in first st. (65)
Rnd 6: Ch 3, dc in next 5 sts, 2 dc in next st, (dc in next 12 sts, 2 dc in next st) 4 times, dc in next 6 sts, join with sl st in first st. (70)
Rnd 7: Ch 3, dc in next 12 sts, 2 dc in next st, (dc in next 13 sts, 2 dc in next st) 4 times, join with sl st in first st. (75)
Rnd 8: Ch 3, dc in next 6 sts, 2 dc in next st, (dc in next 14 sts, 2 dc in next st) 4 times, dc in next 7 sts, join with sl st in first st, changing to **Cassiopeia color white** (one strand). (80)
Rnd 9: Ch 2, hdc in each st around, join with sl st in first st, fasten off. (80)

Sew 3 snap fasteners on the edges of dress, see picture.

Shrug & Scarf

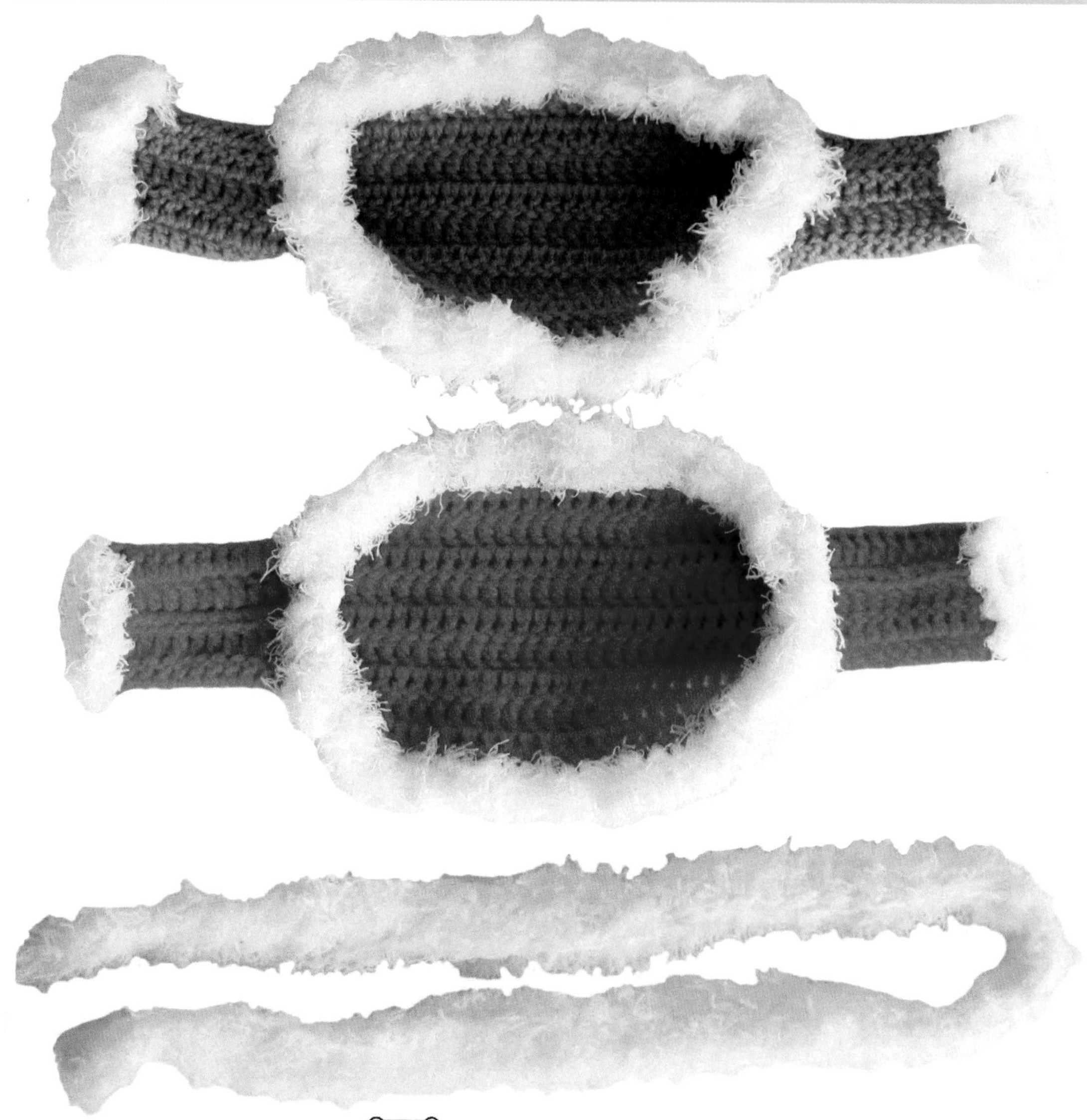

One shrug uses 15 g of DK yarn (DK, Light Worsted).

Robin DK color: Blue Madonna 033 and Red 042

Trim: use 5 g (one shrug) of Chunky yarn

Schachenmayr nomotta Cassiopeia, color: White

Scarf: use 5 g (one scarf) of Chunky yarn

Schachenmayr nomotta Cassiopeia, color: White

Shrug

Working in rows.

Row 1: With one strand of **Red 042** and 4 mm hook, ch 55, dc in 4th chain from hook, dc in next 51 chs, turn. (53)

Row 2-8: Ch 3 (count as one dc), dc in each st across, turn. (53)

Row 9: Ch 3, dc in each st across, leave long end for sewing, fasten off. (53)

Size before folding: 11.8 x 3.6 inches (29.5 x 9 cm).

Fold shrug and sew 2 pieces together about 2.4 inches/ 6 cm from the end.

Edge of shrug (body): With one strand of **Cassiopeia color White** and 4 mm hook, join with sl st, ch 1, sc in same st, (ch 5, sc in next st) around, fasten off.

Edge of shrug (sleeve) With one strand of **Cassiopeia color White** and 4 mm hook; working in end of rows, join with sl st, ch 1, sc in same st, (ch 3, sc in same st, ch 3, sc in next st (next end of row)) around, fasten off.

Diagram of edge of sleeve.

```
  O       O       O
 O O     O O     O O
 X X     X X     X X
  ⊢       ⊢       ⊢     End of rows/
                        edge of
                        sleeve.
                        (Red color)
```

O = ch

X = sc

⊢ = dc

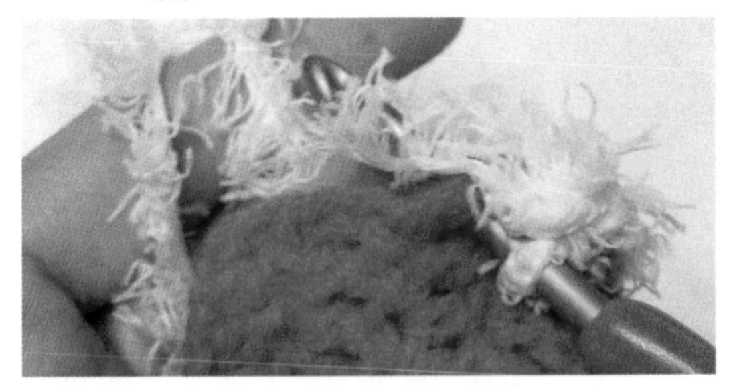

Scarf

Working in rows.

Row 1: With one strand of **Cassiopeia color White** and 5 mm hook, ch 70, sc in 2nd chain from hook, sc in next 68 chs, turn. (69)

Row 2: Ch 1, sc in each st across, fasten off. (69)

Shoulder Straps Dress

One dress uses 16 g of DK yarn (DK, Light Worsted).

Blue dress: Robin DK Royal 086 (15 g) and Turquoise 281 (1 g)
Purple dress: Robin DK Violet 094 (15 g) and Fondant 052 (1 g)

Three 12 mm buttons for one dress.

Shoulder Straps Dress

Working in rows.

Row 1: With one strand of **Royal 086** and 4 mm hook, ch 45, dc in 4th ch from hook, dc in next 41 chs, turn. (ch 3 count as one dc, 43 sts)
Row 2-3: Ch 3(count as one dc), dc in next 42 sts, turn. (43)
Row 4: Ch 3(count as one dc), dc in next 10 sts, 2 dc in next st, dc in next 22 sts, 2 dc in next st, dc in next 8 sts, turn. (45)
Row 5: Ch 3(count as one dc), dc in next 7 sts, 2 dc in next st, (dc in next 8 sts, 2 dc in next st) 4 times, turn. (50)
Row 6: Ch 3(count as one dc), dc in next 8 sts, 2 dc in next st, (dc in next 9 sts, 2 dc in next st) 4 times, turn. (55)
Row 7: Ch 3(count as one dc), dc in next 54 sts, turn. (55)
Row 8: Ch 3(count as one dc), dc in next 9 sts, 2 dc in next st, (dc in next 10 sts, 2 dc in next st) 4 times, turn. (60)
Row 9: Ch 3(count as one dc), dc in next 59 sts, turn. (60)
Row 10: Ch 3(count as one dc), dc in next 10 sts, 2 dc in next st, (dc in next 11 sts, 2 dc in next st) 4 times, turn. (65)
Row 11: Ch 3(count as one dc), dc in next 64 sts, join with sl st in first st, fasten off. (65)

Shoulder straps

With one strand of **Turquoise 281** and 4 mm hook, join yarn to the end of row 1, sc in first 8 sts, ch 10, skip 8 sts, sc in next 10 sts, ch 10, skip 8 sts, sc in next 8 sts, fasten off. (26 sts, 20 chs)

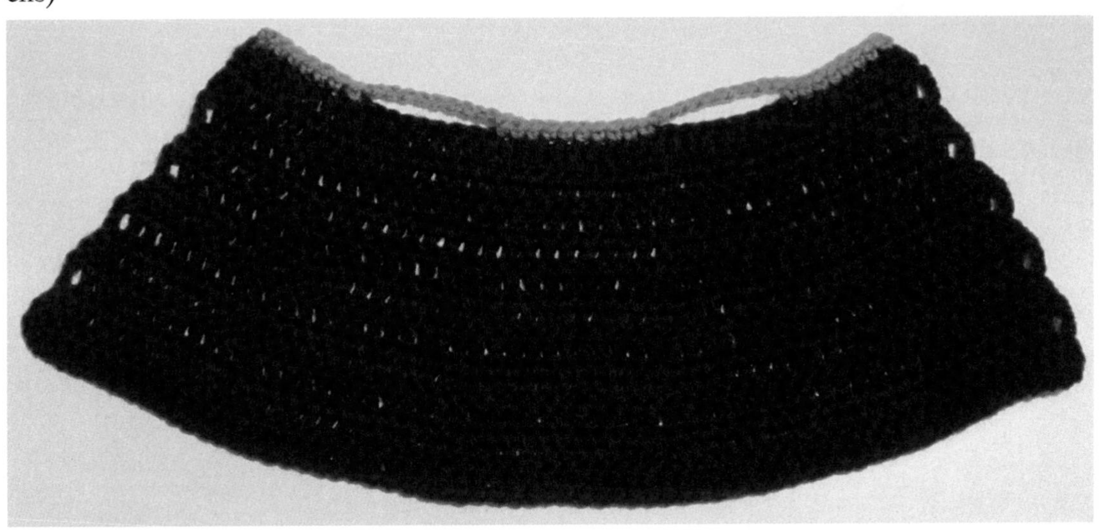

Sew buttons on dress. To button the dress: the buttons go between the dc stitches.

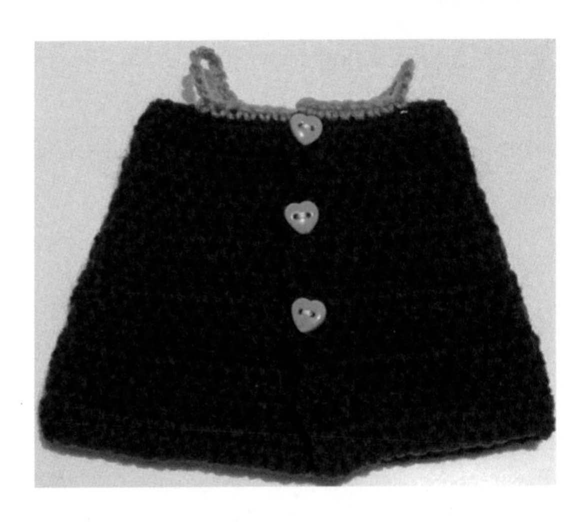

Bell Shaped Dresses

One **Long dress** uses 50 g of DK yarn (DK, Light Worsted).
Robin DK: Pink 046 and Acid Yellow 060
<u>Decoration</u>
Yellow dress: Butterfly trim = 100 cm
Pink dress: Butterfly trim = 100 cm and Lace Frilled color White 28 mm = 70 cm.

One **Short dress** uses 30 g of DK yarn (DK, Light Worsted).
Robin DK: Aqua 130 and White 040
<u>Decoration</u>
White dress: Lace Frilled White 28 mm = 55 cm, 3 mm Red Organza ribbon = 80 cm and one Red bow.
Blue dress: Lace Frilled White 28 mm = 55 cm, 7 mm Blue Ric Rac = 30 cm and one 25 mm Flower button.

Two 5 mm Snap Fasteners or two 12 mm buttons for each dress.

Bell Shaped Long Dress

Working in rows.
Row 1: With one strand of **Pink 046** and 4 mm hook, ch 38, dc in 4th chain from hook, dc in next 3 chs, 2 dc in next ch, (dc in next 5 chs, 2 dc in next ch) 5 times, turn. (ch 3 count as one dc, 42)
Row 2: Ch 3(count as one dc), dc in next 5 sts, 2 dc in next st, (dc in next 6 sts, 2dc in next st) 5 times, turn. (48)
Row 3: Ch 3(count as one dc), dc in next 47 sts, turn. (48)
Row 4: Ch 3 (count as one dc), dc in next 5 sts, ch 6, skip 10 sts, dc in next 16 sts, ch 6, skip 10 sts, dc in next 6 sts, turn. (28 sts, 12 chs)

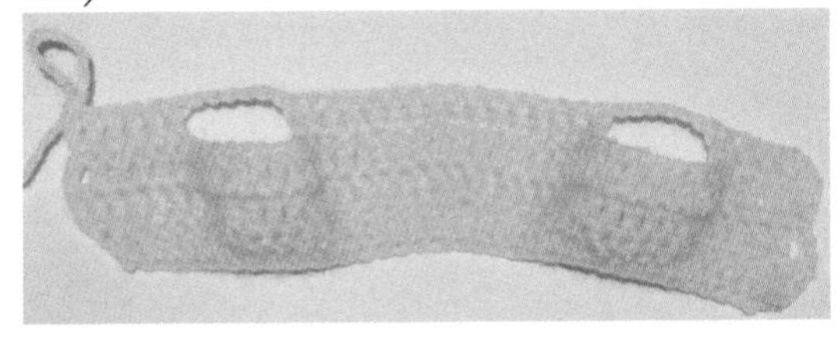

Row 5: Ch 3 (count as one dc), dc in next 5 sts, dc in next 6 chs, dc in next 16 sts, dc in next 6 chs, dc in next 6 sts, turn. (40)
Row 6: Ch 3 (count as one dc), dc in next 39 sts, turn. (40)

Rnds 7 - 25 are working in rounds and join with sl st at the end of round.
Rnd 7: Ch 3 (count as one dc), dc in next 37 sts, skip 2 sts, join with sl st in first st. (38)
Rnd 8: Ch 3 (count as one dc), 2 dc in next st, (dc in next st, 2 dc in next st) around, join with sl st in first st. (57)
Rnd 9: Ch 3 (count as one dc), dc in next st, 2 dc in next st, (dc in next 2 sts, 2 dc in next st) around, join with sl st in first st. (76)
Rnd 10: Ch 3 (count as one dc), dc in next 17 sts, 2 dc in next st, (dc in next 18 sts, 2 dc in next st) 3 times, join with sl st in first st. (80)
Rnd 11: Ch 3(count as one dc), dc in next 79 sts, join with sl st in first st. (80)
Rnd 12: Ch 3 (count as one dc), dc in next 14 sts, 2 dc in next st, (dc in next 15 sts, 2 dc in next st) 4 times, join with sl st in first st. (85)
Rnd 13: Ch 3(count as one dc), dc in next 84 sts, join with sl st in first st. (85)
Rnd 14: Ch 3 (count as one dc), dc in next 15 sts, 2 dc in next st, (dc in next 16 sts, 2 dc in next st) 4 times, join with sl st in first st. (90)
Rnd 15: Ch 3(count as one dc), dc in next 89 sts, join with sl st in first st. (90)
Rnd 16: Ch 3 (count as one dc), dc in next 16 sts, 2 dc in next st, (dc in next 17 sts, 2 dc in next st) 4 times, join with sl st in first st. (95)
Rnd 17: Ch 3(count as one dc), dc in next 94 sts, join with sl st in first st. (95)
Rnd 18: Ch 3 (count as one dc), dc in next 17 sts, 2 dc in next st, (dc in next 18 sts, 2 dc in next st) 4 times, join with sl st in first st. (100)
Rnd 19: Ch 3(count as one dc), dc in next 99 sts, join with sl st in first st. (100)
Rnd 20: Ch 3 (count as one dc), dc in next 18 sts, 2 dc in next st, (dc in next 19 sts, 2 dc in next st) 4 times, join with sl st in first st. (105)
Rnd 21: Ch 3(count as one dc), dc in next 104 sts, join with sl st in first st. (105)
Rnd 22: Ch 3 (count as one dc), dc in next 19 sts, 2 dc in next st, (dc in next 20 sts, 2 dc in next st) 4 times, join with sl st in first st. (110)

Rnd 23: Ch 3(count as one dc), dc in next 109 sts, join with sl st in first st. (110)
Rnd 24: Ch 3 (count as one dc), dc in next 20 sts, 2 dc in next st, (dc in next 21 sts, 2 dc in next st) 4 times, join with sl st in first st. (115)
Rnd 25: Ch 3(count as one dc), dc in next 114 sts, join with sl st in first st, fasten off. (115)

Sew snap fasteners on the dress (mark X), see picture.

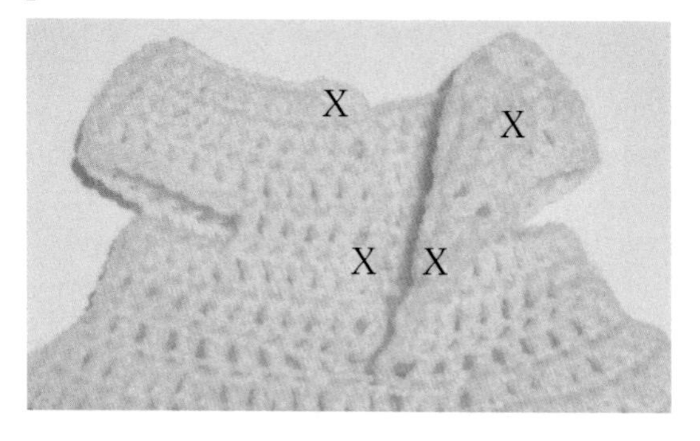

Pink dress: Sew butterfly trim and lace on the last row of dress (row 25). Cut butterfly off from butterfly trim and sew randomly on dress.

Or sew buttons as in picture below.
To button the dress: the buttons go between the dc stitches.

Yellow dress: Sew butterfly trim on the last row of dress (row 25) and cut butterfly off from butterfly trim and sew randomly on dress.

Bell Shaped Short Dress

Same as Long dress pattern but fasten off after row 17.

Blue dress: Weave the Blue Ric Rac between the stitches in row 7 and sew both ends to row 7. Sew Flower button in the front on row 7.

White dress: Weave the Red Organza ribbon between the stitches in row 7 and sew both
ends of ribbon to row 7. Sew Red bow in the front on row 7.

Weave the Red Organza ribbon between the stitches in row 17 and sew both ends of ribbon together. Sew lace on the last row of dress (row 17).

Red Riding Hood Cape

One hood uses 32 g of DK yarn (DK, Light Worsted).

Robin DK color Red 042

Cape

Working in rows.

Row 1: With one strand of **Red 042** and 4 mm hook, ch 45, dc in 4th ch from hook, dc in next 41 chs, turn. (ch 3 couthnt as one dc, 43 sts)

Row 2-3: Ch 3(count as one dc), dc in next 42 sts, turn. (43)

Row 4: Ch 3(count as one dc), dc in next 10 sts, 2 dc in next st, dc in next 22 sts, 2 dc in next st, dc in next 8 sts, turn. (45)

Row 5: Ch 3(count as one dc), dc in next 7 sts, 2 dc in next st, (dc in next 8 sts, 2 dc in next st) 4 times, turn. (50)

Row 6: Ch 3(count as one dc), dc in next 8 sts, 2 dc in next st, (dc in next 9 sts, 2 dc in next st) 4 times, turn. (55)

Row 7: Ch 3(count as one dc), dc in next 54 sts, turn. (55)

Row 8: Ch 3(count as one dc), dc in next 9 sts, 2 dc in next st, (dc in next 10 sts, 2 dc in next st) 4 times, turn. (60)

Row 9: Ch 3(count as one dc), dc in next 59 sts, turn. (60)

Row 10: Ch 3(count as one dc), dc in next 10 sts, 2 dc in next st, (dc in next 11 sts, 2 dc in next st) 4 times, turn. (65)

Row 11: Ch 3(count as one dc), dc in next 64 sts, join with sl st in first st, fasten off. (65)

Cape after finished row 11.

Strap
With one strand of **Red 042** and 4 mm hook, ch 30, sc in each st on row 1 of Cape, ch 30, fasten off. (ch 60, 43 sts)

Hood

Working in rows.

Row 1: With one strand of **Red 042** and 4 mm hook, ch 60, dc in 4th chain from hook, dc in next 56 chs, turn. (ch 3 count as one dc, 58)

Row 2-9: Ch 3(count as one dc), dc in next 57 sts, turn. (58)

Row 10: Ch 3(count as one dc), dc in next 17 sts, (dc next 2 sts tog) 11 times, dc in next 18 sts, turn. (47)

Row 11: Ch 3(count as one dc), dc in next 9 sts, (dc next 2 sts tog) 6 times, dc next 3 sts tog, (dc next 2 sts tog) 6 times, dc in next 10 sts, turn. (33)

Row 12: Ch 3(count as one dc), dc in next 32 sts, turn. (33)

Row 13: Ch 1, sc in first st, sc in next 4 sts, hdc in next st, (dc next 2 sts tog) 5 times, dc in next st, (dc next 2 sts tog) 5 times, hdc in next st, sc in next 5 sts, leave long end for sewing, fasten off. (23)

Sew row 13 together.

Pin Hood and Cape together as in picture.

Sew Hood to Cape.

Uniform

White Top

One top uses 15 g of DK yarn (DK, Light Worsted).

Robin DK color White 040

Boy & Girl have same white top.

Front

Row 1: With one strand of **White 040** and 4 mm hook, ch 28, dc in 4th chain from hook, dc in next 24 chs, turn. (ch 3 count as one dc, 26 sts)

Row 2-6: Ch 3(count as one dc), dc in next 25 sts, turn. (26)

Row 7: Ch 1, sc each st across, turn. (26)

Row 8: Ch 1, sc in first st, sc in next 19 sts, turn. (20)

Row 9: Ch 7, sc in second chain from hook, sc in next 5 chs, sc in next 20 sts, turn. (26)

Row 10-14: Ch 3(count as one dc), dc in next 25 sts, turn. (26)

Row 15: Ch 3(count as one dc), dc in next 25 sts, fasten off. (26)

Back

Row 1: With one strand of **White 040** and 4 mm hook, ch 28, dc in 4th chain from hook, dc in next 24 chs, turn. (ch 3 count as one dc, 26)

Row 2-4: Ch 3(count as one dc), dc in next 25 sts, turn. (26)

Row 5-9: Ch 3(count as one dc), dc in next 22 sts, turn. (23)

Row 10: Ch 5, dc in 4th chain from hook, dc in next ch, dc in next 23 sts, turn. (ch 3 count as one dc, 26 sts)

Row 11-12: Ch 3(count as one dc), dc in next 25 sts, turn. (26)

Row 13: Ch 3(count as one dc), dc in next 25 sts, fasten off. (26)

Sew 2 pieces together:

Shoulders: sew 4 rows from the edge.

Sew both sides of body and leave 1.6 inches/ 4 cm for arm holes.

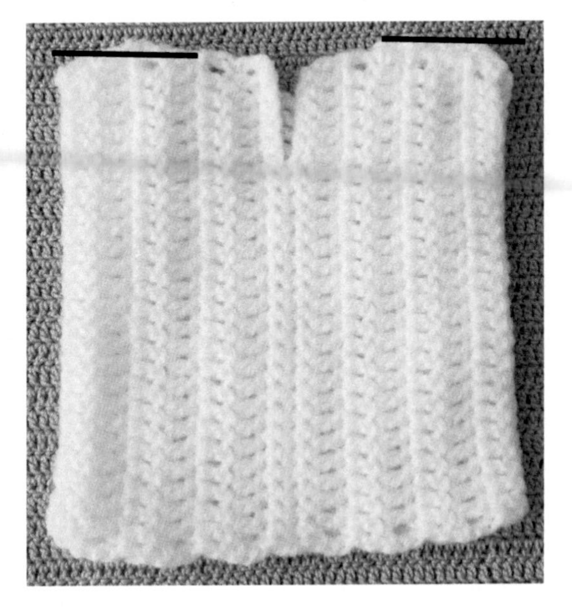

Skirt

One skirt uses 20 g of DK yarn (DK, Light Worsted).

Robin DK color Black 044

Two 5 mm Snap fasteners.

Skirt

Rnd 1: With one strand of **Black 044** and 4 mm hook, ch 50, sl st in first ch to form a ring, ch 3 (count as one dc), dc in next 49 chs, join with sl st in first st. (50)
Rnd 2-3: Ch 3(count as one dc), dc in next 49 sts, join with sl st in first st. (50)
Rnd 4: Ch 3(count as one dc), dc in next 8 sts, 2 dc in next st, (dc in next 9 sts, 2 dc in next st) 4 times, join with sl st in first st. (55)
Rnd 5: Ch 3(count as one dc), dc in next 54 sts, join with sl st in first st. (55)
Rnd 6: Ch 3(count as one dc), dc in next 9 sts, 2 dc in next st, (dc in next 10 sts, 2 dc in next st) 4 times, join with sl st in first st. (60)
Rnd 7: Ch 3(count as one dc), dc in next 59 sts, join with sl st in first st. (60)
Rnd 8: Ch 3(count as one dc), dc in next 10 sts, 2 dc in next st, (dc in next 11 sts, 2 dc in next st) 4 times, join with sl st in first st. (65)
Rnd 9: Ch 3(count as one dc), dc in next 64 sts, join with sl st in first st, fasten off. (65)

Waist

Rnd 1: With one strand of **Black 044** and 4 mm hook, join yarn to Round 1 of skirt, ch 1, sc in same st, sc in next 49 sts, join with sl st in first st. (50)
Rnd 2: Ch 1, sc in each st around, join with sl st in first st, fasten off. (50)

Strap

Make 2.

Row 1: With one strand of **Black 044** and 4 mm hook, ch 35, sc in second chain from hook, sc in next 33 chs, leave long end for sewing, fasten off. (34)

Sew straps on the front as in picture.

Sew snap fasteners on the straps and on the back of skirt.

Shorts

One pants uses 20 g of DK yarn (DK, Light Worsted).

Robin DK color Black 044

One 5 mm Snap fastener.

Shorts

Rnd 1: With one strand of **Black 044** and 4 mm hook, ch 50, sl st in first ch to form a ring, ch 3 (count as one dc), dc in next 49 chs, join with sl st in first st. (50)
Rnd 2-5: Ch 3(count as one dc), dc in next 49 sts, join with sl st in first st. (50)
Rnd 6: Start first leg; ch 3 (count as one dc), dc in next 24 sts, skip next 25 sts, join with sl st in first st. (25)
Rnd 7-9: Ch 3 (count as one dc), dc in next 24 sts, join with sl st in first st. (25)
Rnd 10: Ch 3 (count as one dc), dc in next 24 sts, join with sl st in first st, fasten off. (25)

Rnd 6: Start second leg; With one strand of **Black 044** and 4 mm hook, join yarn to next free st on rnd 5, ch 3 (count as one dc), dc in next 24 sts, join with sl st in first st. (25)
Rnd 7-9: Ch 3 (count as one dc), dc in next 24 sts, join with sl st in first st. (25)
Rnd 10: Ch 3 (count as one dc), dc in next 24 sts, join with sl st in first st, fasten off. (25)

Waist

Working in rows.
Row 1: With one strand of **Black 044** and 4 mm hook, join yarn to middle front of shorts, ch 3 (count as one dc), dc in next 49 sts, turn. (50)
Row 2: Ch 4, sc in second chain from hook, sc in next 2 chs, sc in next 50 sts, turn. (53)
Row 3: Ch 1, sc in first st, sc in next 52 sts, fasten off. (53)

Sew the opening at crotch close.

Sew snap fastener as in picture.

Top & Trousers

Blue Top

One top uses 17 g of DK yarn (DK, Light Worsted).

Robin DK color Royal(blue) 086

Top

Make 2. Working in rows.

Row 1: With one strand of **Royal 086** and 4 mm hook, ch 28, dc in 4th chain from hook, dc in next 24 chs, turn. (ch 3 count as one dc, 26)

Row 2-4: Ch 3(count as one dc), dc in next 25 sts, turn. (26)

Row 5-9: Ch 3(count as one dc), dc in next 22 sts, turn. (23)

Row 10: Ch 5, dc in 4th chain from hook, dc in next ch, dc in next 23 sts, turn. (ch 3 count as one dc, 26 sts)

Row 11-12: Ch 3(count as one dc), dc in next 25 sts, turn. (26)

Row 13: Ch 3(count as one dc), dc in next 25 sts, fasten off. (26)

Sew 2 pieces together: Shoulders sew 4 rows from the edge. Sew both sides of body and leave 1.6 inches/ 4 cm for arm hole.

Trousers

One trousers uses 15 g of DK yarn (DK, Light Worsted).
Robin DK color Taupe 093

One 5 mm Snap fastener.

Trousers
Rnd 1: With one strand of **Taupe 093** and 4 mm hook, ch 50, sl st in first ch to form ring, ch 3 (count as one dc), dc in next 49 chs, join with sl st in first st. (50)
Rnd 2-5: Ch 3(count as one dc), dc in next 49 chs, join with sl st in first st. (50)
Rnd 6: Start first leg; ch 3 (count as one dc), dc in next 24 sts, skip next 25 sts, join with sl st in first st. (25)
Rnd 7-16: Ch 3 (count as one dc), dc in next 24 sts, join with sl st in first st. (25)
Rnd 17: Ch 3 (count as one dc), dc in next 24 sts, join with sl st in first st, fasten off. (25)

Rnd 6: Start second leg; With one strand of **Taupe 093** and 4 mm hook, join yarn to next free st on rnd 5, ch 3 (count as one dc), dc in next 24 sts, join with sl st in first st. (25)
Rnd 7-16: Ch 3 (count as one dc), dc in next 24 sts, join with sl st in first st. (25)
Rnd 17: Ch 3 (count as one dc), dc in next 24 sts, join with sl st in first st, fasten off. (25)

Sew the opening at crotch close.

Waist
Working in rows.
Row 1: With one strand of **Taupe 093** and 4 mm hook, join yarn to middle front of trousers, ch 3 (count as one dc), dc in next 49 sts, turn. (50)
Row 2: Ch 4, sc in second chain from hook, sc in next 2 chs, sc in next 50 sts, turn. (53)
Row 3: Ch 1, sc in first st, sc in next 52 sts, fasten off. (53)

Sew snap fastener as in picture.

Jacket

One jacket uses 27 g of DK yarn (DK, Light Worsted).

Robin DK color Silver 027 and Taupe 093

Front

Make 2. Working in rows.

Row 1: With one strand of **Taupe 093** and 4 mm hook, ch 33, dc in 4th chain from hook, dc in next 29 chs, turn. (ch 3 count as one dc, 31 sts)

Row 2-4: Ch 3(count as one dc), dc in next 30 sts, turn. (31)

Row 5-8: Ch 3(count as one dc), dc in next 27 sts, turn. (28)

Row 9: Ch 3(count as one dc), dc in next 27 sts, fasten off. (28)

Back

Working in rows.

Row 1: With one strand of **Taupe 093** and 4 mm hook, ch 33, dc in 4th chain from hook, dc in next 29 chs, turn. (ch 3 count as one dc, 31 sts)

Row 2-4: Ch 3(count as one dc), dc in next 30 sts, turn. (31)

Row 5-9: Ch 3(count as one dc), dc in next 27 sts, turn. (28)

Row 10: Ch 5, dc in 4th chain from hook, dc in next ch, dc in next 28 sts, turn. (ch 3 count as one dc, 31 sts)

Row 11-12: Ch 3(count as one dc), dc in next 30 sts, turn. (31)

Row 13: Ch 3(count as one dc), dc in next 30 sts, fasten off. (31)

Sleeve

Make 2. Working in rows.

Row 1: With one strand of **Taupe 093** and 4 mm hook, ch 20, dc in 4th chain from hook, dc in next 16 chs, turn. (ch 3 count as one dc, 18 sts)

Row 2-3: Ch 3(count as one dc), dc in next 17 sts, turn. (18)

Row 4: Ch 3(count as one dc), dc in next 17 sts, fasten off. (18)

Taupe jacket has 3/4 length sleeves (4 rows). Silver jacket has long sleeves (5 rows: row 5 is same as row 4).

Sew shoulder of fronts and back together then sew sleeves as in picture below.

Sew both sides of body and sleeves together.

Doll Bags

Messenger Bag

One bag uses 10 g of DK yarn (DK, Light Worsted). 3 Light
Robin DK: Taupe 093 and Fiesta 064

Two 12 mm Buttons for one bag.

Rnd 1: Working around starting chain. With one strand of **Taupe 093** and 4 mm hook, ch 15, dc in 4th chain from hook, dc in next 10 chs, 3 dc in next ch; working in remaining loops on opposite side of chain, dc in next 11 chs, 2 dc in next ch, join with sl st in first st. (28)

Rnd 2-5: Ch 3 (count as one dc), dc in next 27 sts, join with sl st in first st. (28)

Rows 6-9 are working in rows.
Row 6-8: Ch 3 (count as one dc), dc in next 12 sts, turn. (13)
Row 9: Ch 3 (count as one dc), dc in next 12 sts, fasten off. (13)

Strap
Row 1: With one strand of **Taupe 093** and 4 mm hook, ch 55, sc in second chain from hook, sc in next 53 chs, leave long end for sewing, fasten off. (54)

Sew straps and buttons to the bag as in picture. The buttons go in between the dc stitches on row 9 of bag.

Square Handbag

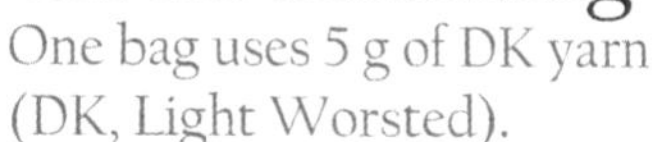

One bag uses 5 g of DK yarn (DK, Light Worsted).
Robin DK: Turquoise 281 and Fondant 052

One 25 mm Flower Button for each bag.

Rnd 1-5: Same as messenger bag on page 79.
Rnd 6: Ch 3 (count as one dc), dc in next 27 sts, join with sl st in first st. (28)
Rnd 7: Ch 1, sc in first st, sc in next 3 sts, ch 10, skip 6 sts, sc in next 8 sts, ch 10, skip 6 sts, sc in next 4 sts, join with sl st in first st, fasten off. (16 sts, 20 chs)

Sew Flower Button on bag for decoration.

Circle Handbag

One bag uses 5 g of DK yarn (DK, Light Worsted).
Robin DK: Aqua 130 and Red 042

One 25 mm Flower Buttons for one bag.
20 of 5 mm White beads for making handle.

Make 2.
Rnd 1: With 2 strands of **Aqua 130** and 5 mm hook, ch 2, 6 sc in second chain from hook. (6)
Rnd 2: 2 sc in each st around. (12)
Rnd 3: (2 sc in next st, sc in next st) around, join with sl st in first st, fasten off. (18)

Sew Flower button on the middle of one circle.

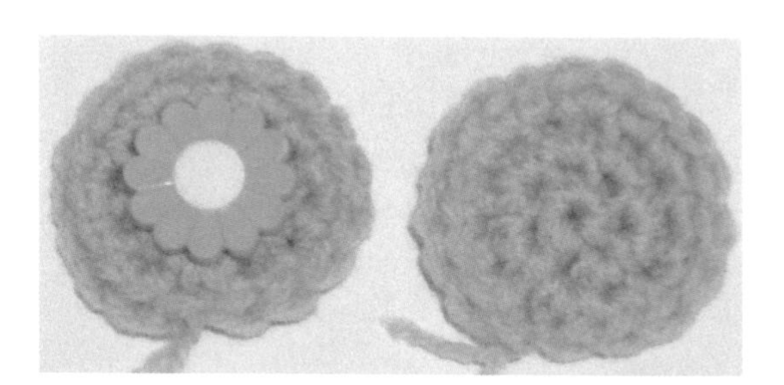

Sew 2 pieces together: do not sew 5 sts for the opening of the bag. String beads for the handle.

Beach Bag

One bag uses 15 g of DK yarn (DK, Light Worsted).
Bottom (dark color) uses 4 g
Body (light color) uses 11 g
Robin DK color:

- Fondant 052 and Pink 046
- Jaffa 063 and Peach 049
- Cordial 162 and Spearmint 057
- Turquoise 281 and Pale Blue 047

Rnd 1: With two strands of **Fondant 052** and 5 mm hook, ch 2, 6 sc in second chain from hook. (6)
Rnd 2: 2 sc in each st around. (12)
Rnd 3: (2 sc in next st, sc in next st) around. (18)
Rnd 4: (Sc in next 2 sts, 2 sc in next st) around. (24)
Rnd 5: (Sc in next 3 sts, 2 sc in next st) around, changing to **Pink 046** in last 2 loops of last st. (30)
Rnd 6-13: Sc in each st around. (30)
Rnd 14: Sc in next 4 sts, ch 15, skip 7 sts, sc in next 8 sts, ch 15, skip 7 sts, sc in next 4 sts. (16 sts, 30 chs)
Rnd 15: Sl st in next 4 sts, sl st in next 15 chs, sl st in next 8 sts, sl st in next 15 chs, sl st in next 4 sts, fasten off. (46)

Watering Can

Watering Can

One watering can uses 12 g of DK yarn (DK, Light Worsted).

3 Light

Robin DK: Cordial(green) 162 and Jaffa(orange) 063

Part 1

Rnd 1: With two strands of **Cordial 162** and 5 mm hook, ch 2, 6 sc in second chain from hook. (6)
Rnd 2: 2 sc in each st around. (12)
Rnd 3: (Sc in next st, 2 sc in next st) around. (18)
Rnd 4: (2 sc in next st, sc in next 2 sts) around. (24)
Rnd 5: Working in back loops only. Sc in each st around.
Rnd 6-10: Sc in each st around.
Rnd 11: Sc in each st around, join with sl st in first st, start the handle; ch 10, skip 12 sts, join with sl st in next st, sl st in each ch across, join with sl st in first st. Fasten off.

Part 2

Rnd 1: Ch 2, 6 sc in second chain from hook. (6)
Rnd 2: 2 sc in each st around. (12)
Rnd 3: Working in back loops only. (Sc next 2 sts tog) around.(6)
Rnd 4: Sc in each st around. (6)
Rnd 5: Sc next 2 sts tog around, join with sl st in first st. Fasten off. (3)

Assembly: Sew rnd 5 of part 2 over rnd 7-8 of part 1.

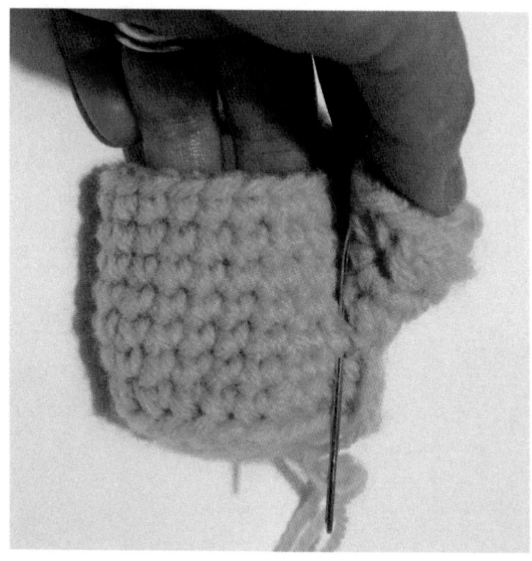

Big Carry Bag

Size

Big Bag: Bottom diameter 9.5 inches /24 cm

Use 6 mm hook and chunky yarn
Dark color 40 g and Pale color 140 g.
Hayfield Bonus Chunky color Bubblegum 776
Robin Chunky color Pink 046

5 Bulky

Small Bag: Bottom diameter 8.7 inches /22 cm

Use 5 mm hook and 2 strands of DK yarn
Dark color 35 g and Pale color 130 g.
Robin Chunky color Cordial 162 and
Acid Yellow 060

3 Light

Bag

Rnd 1: With **Dark color** (bottom color), ch 2, 6 sc in second chain from hook. (6)
Rnd 2: 2 sc in each st around. (12)
Rnd 3: (2 sc in next st, sc in next st) around. (18)
Rnd 4: (Sc in next 2 sts, 2 sc in next st) around. (24)
Rnd 5: (Sc in next 3 sts, 2 sc in next st) around. (30)
Rnd 6: Sc in next 2 sts, 2 sc in next st, (sc in next 4 sts, 2 sc in next st) 5 times, sc in next 2 sts. (36)
Rnd 7: (Sc in next 5 sts, 2 sc in next st) around. (42)
Rnd 8: Sc in next 3 sts, 2 sc in next st, (sc in next 6 sts, 2 sc in next st) 5 times, sc in next 3 sts. (48)
Rnd 9: (Sc in next 7 sts, 2 sc in next st) around. (54)
Rnd 10: Sc in next 4 sts, 2 sc in next st, (sc in next 8 sts, 2 sc in next st) 5 times, sc in next 4 sts. (60)
Rnd 11: (Sc in next 9 sts, 2 sc in next st) around. (66)
Rnd 12: Sc in next 5 sts, 2 sc in next st, (sc in next 10 sts, 2 sc in next st) 5 times, sc in next 5 sts. (72)
Rnd 13: (Sc in next 11 sts, 2 sc in next st) around. (78)
Rnd 14: Sc in next 6 sts, 2 sc in next st, (sc in next 12 sts, 2 sc in next st) 5 times, sc in next 6 sts. (84)
Rnd 15: (Sc in next 13 sts, 2 sc in next st) around. (90)
Rnd 16: Sc in next 7 sts, 2 sc in next st, (sc in next 14 sts, 2 sc in next st) 5 times, sc in next 7 sts. (96)
Rnd 17: (Sc in next 15 sts, 2 sc in next st) around, changing to **Light color** (body color) in last 2 loops of last st. (102)
Rnd 18-44: Sc in each st around. (102)
Rnd 45: Sc in next 15 sts, ch 50, skip 21 sts, sc in next 30 sts, ch 50, skip 21 sts, sc in next 15 sts, join with sl st in first st. (60 sts, 100 chs)
Rnd 46: Ch 3 (count as one dc), dc next 2 sts tog, (dc in next st, dc next 2 sts tog) 4 times, (dc next 2 chs tog) 3 times, dc in next 38 chs, (dc next 2 chs tog) 3 times, (dc next 2 sts tog, dc in next st) 5 times, (dc in next st, dc next 2 sts tog) 5 times, (dc next 2 chs tog) 3 times, dc in next 38 chs, (dc next 2 chs tog) 3 times, (dc next 2 sts tog, dc in next st) 5 times, sl st in first st. (128)
Rnd 47: Ch 3 (count as one dc), 2 dc in next st, (dc in next st, 2 dc in next st) 4 times, 2 dc in next 3 sts, dc in next [illegible] 2 dc in next 3 sts, (2 dc in next [illegible]) 5 times, (dc in next st, 2 [illegible] times, 2 dc in next 3 sts, dc in [illegible] sts, 2 dc in next 3 sts, (2 dc in next st, dc in next st) 5 times, sl st in first st, leave long end for sewing (135 cm), fasten off. (160)

Fold the last round and sew as in pictures below.

How to join Yarn.

Join yarn to free loop, ch 1, sc in same st.

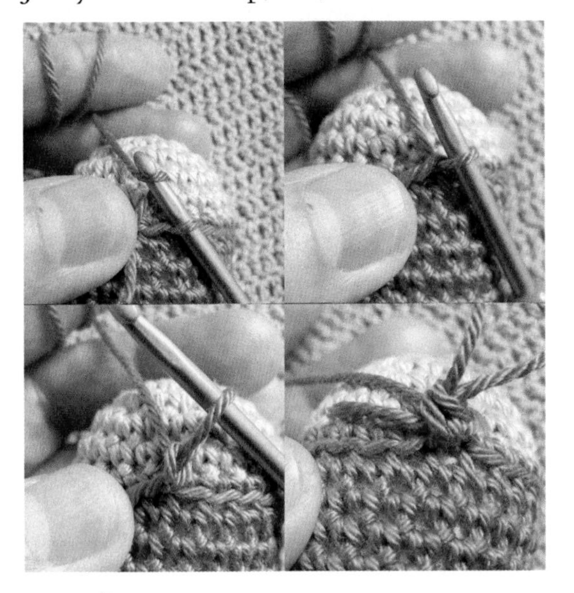

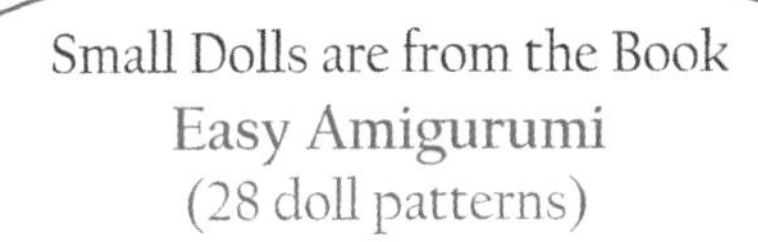

How to read pattern.

Rnd 4: (Sc in next 2 sts, 2 sc in next st) around. (24)

Number (24) at the end of round = number of stitches after finished round.

Rnd 5: (Sc in next 3 sts, 2 sc in next st) **around. (30)**

Repeat (Sc in next 3 sts, 2 sc in next st) until end of round

=> **Rnd 5:** (Sc in next 3 sts, 2 sc in next st), (Sc in next 3 sts, 2 sc in next st), (Sc in next 3 sts, 2 sc in next st), (Sc in next 3 sts, 2 sc in next st), (Sc in next 3 sts, 2 sc in next st), (Sc in next 3 sts, 2 sc in next st)

Total stitches of Rnd 5 = 5+5+5+5+5+5 = 30 sts

Rnd 6: Sc in next 2 sts, 2 sc in next st, (sc in next 4 sts, 2 sc in next st) 5 times, **sc in next 2 sts. (36)**

Repeat (sc in next 4 sts, 2 sc in next st) 5 times

=> **Rnd 6: Sc in next 2 sts, 2 sc in next st,** (sc in next 4 sts, 2 sc in next st), (sc in next 4 sts, 2 sc in next st), (sc in next 4 sts, 2 sc in next st), (sc in next 4 sts, 2 sc in next st), (sc in next 4 sts, 2 sc in next st), **sc in next 2 sts.**

Total stitches of Rnd 6 = 2+2+6+6+6+6+6+2 = 36 sts

Follow Sayjai on www.facebook.com/kandjdolls.amigurumi.patterns
kandjdolls.blogspot.com for new Dresses & Accessories

Yarn Weight System

USA		UK	Australia	Recommended Hook in Metric (mm)
0 Lace	Lace weight	1 ply	2 ply	1.5 - 2.25 mm
1 Super fine	Fingering	2 ply	3 ply	2.25 - 3 mm
	Sock	3 ply	3 ply	2.25 - 3.5 mm
2 Fine	Sport	4 ply	5 ply	3.5 - 4.5 mm
3 Light	DK Light worsted	DK	8 ply	4.5 - 5.5 mm
4 Medium	Worsted	Aran	10 ply	5.5 - 6.5 mm
5 Bulky	Bulky	Chunky	12 ply	6.5 - 9 mm
6 Super Bulky	Super Bulky	Super Chunky	14 ply	9 mm and larger

Crochet Hook Size Conversion			
Hook in Metric (mm)	USA	UK	Japanese
1.00 mm	10 steel	4 steel	4 steel
1.25 mm	8 steel	3 steel	2 steel
1.50 mm	7 steel	2.5 steel	--
1.75 mm	4 steel	2 steel	--
2.00 mm	--	14	2/0
2.25 mm	B/1	13	3/0
2.50 mm	--	12	4/0
2.75 mm	C/2	--	--
3.00 mm	--	11	5/0
3.25 mm	D/3	10	--
3.50 mm	E/4	9	6/0
3.75 mm	F/5	--	--
4.00 mm	G/6	8	7/0
4.50 mm	7	7	7.5/0
5.00 mm	H/8	6	8/0
5.50 mm	I/9	5	--
6.00 mm	J/10	4	10/0
6.50 mm	K/10.5	3	7
7.00 mm	--	2	--
8.00 mm	L/11	0	8
9.00 mm	M/13	00	9
10.00 mm	N/15	000	10

Copyright

First Edition
Date of publication: 27th of September 2014
Editor: Robert Appelboom
Publisher: K and J Publishing
Cambridge, England

This is the third volume in "Sayjai's Amigurumi Crochet Patterns" series.
Below are volume 1 and 2 which can be ordered at your local or online bookstore:

Easy Amigurumi
Subtitle: 28 doll patterns
Publisher: K and J Publishing
Author: Sayjai Thawornsupacharoen
Publication date: 18th of July 2014
ISBN: 978-1910407011

Huggy Dolls Amigurumi
Subtitle: 15 Huggable Doll Patterns
Publisher: K and J Publishing
Author: Sayjai Thawornsupacharoen
Publication date: 14th of June 2014
ISBN: 978-1910407028